MARCO

Inside
Tips

HAMBURG

DENMARK

Heligoland · Fehmarn

Schleswig-
Holstein

North Sea

Hamburg · Mecklenburg-
Vorpommern

Bremen · *Elbe* Brandenburg

Weser

Lower Saxony

Hanover Saxony-
Anhalt

North Rhine- Magdeburg
Westphalia

The best Insider Tips → p. 4

INSIDER TIP

Best of ... → p. 6

Sightseeing → p. 26

Food & Drink → p. 60

SYMBOLS

INSIDER TIP	Insider Tip
★	Highlight
●●●●	Best of ...
⚘	Scenic view
☺	Responsible travel: fair trade principles and the environment respected

PRICE CATEGORIES HOTELS

Expensive over 160 euros

Moderate 110–160 euros

Budget under 110 euros

Rates are for two people including breakfast in a double room

PRICE CATEGORIES RESTAURANTS

Expensive over 25 euros

Moderate 15–25 euros

Budget under 15 euros

The prices are for an average main course without drinks

On the cover: From the Speicherstadt to HafenCity p. 42 | Night turns to day p. 80

CONTENTS

Shopping → p. 72

Entertainment → p. 80

Where to stay → p. 90

Street atlas → p. 122

DID YOU KNOW?

The lowlands? No way!
→ p. 14
Out on the water→ p. 20
Relax & Enjoy → p. 35
Books & Films → p. 52
Gourmet restaurants → p. 64
Local specialities → p. 68
City of sport? Yes! → p. 84
Luxury hotels → p. 94
Budgeting → p. 114
Weather in Hamburg → p. 115

MAPS IN THE GUIDEBOOK

(124 A1) Page numbers and coordinates refer to the street atlas and road atlas of surrounds
Coordinates are also given for places that are not marked on the street atlas
A public transportation map can be found inside the back cover

INSIDE BACK COVER:
PULL-OUT MAP →

PULL-OUT MAP 🗺

(🗺 A–B 2–3) Refers to the removable pull-out map

The best MARCO POLO Insider Tips

Our top 15 Insider Tips

INSIDER TIP Chic and colourful

With its many old buildings, maze of streets, squares, shops, traditional pubs and hip hangouts, *Ottensen* is one of Hamburg's most popular districts → p. 51

INSIDER TIP Meese meets visitors

Jonathan Meese's eccentric artistic creations can be admired in the galleries of the *Sammlung Falckenberg* in Harburg, by prior arrangement only but it is well worth it → p. 58

INSIDER TIP A bit of an oddity

Punks, mothers and canvassers with clipboards all congregate here at *Park Fiction* in St Pauli under plastic palm trees to play basketball or have a beer (photo right) → p. 40

INSIDER TIP View from the bunker

The view from the *Energiebunker* extends well beyond the Elbe island of Wilhelmsburg. You can also enjoy coffee and cake on the café terrace and there is information about the Garden Show → p. 23

INSIDER TIP Cakes to die for

The whole Schanzenviertel (photo above) is a trendy area, but the *Herr Max* café outdoes them all: cakes and petits fours decorated with grinning skulls or skeletons – they look amazing and they're also delicious → p. 62

INSIDER TIP Outdoor theatre

Hamburg does its own 'Jedermann' – the classic Everyman fable – a superb open-air production in the Speicherstadt → p. 44, 109

INSIDER TIP One time around

With the bright red boats of the *Maritime Circle Line* you can travel across the harbour to the former 'emigration port' of Ballinstadt → p. 57

INSIDER TIP Lunch break at Bodo's

Sink into a deckchair at *Bodo's Bootssteg* on the Alster – that's the life. And afterwards you can always hire a rowing boat → p. 62

INSIDER TIP Culture in the attic

The *Nachtasyl* at the Thalia Theatre, high up in the roof of the old building on Gerhart-Hauptmann-Platz, is one of Hamburg's trendiest bars with a regular programme of live shows → p. 88

INSIDER TIP Tango by the river

With its dance floor the banks of the Elbe, atmospheric torches lit and ice clinking in the caipirinha glasses, there is no better way to spend a summer evening than doing a tango at the *Strandpauli* beach club in St Pauli → p. 83

INSIDER TIP Fish and cards

In the well-established lunchtime restaurant *Zum Steckelhörn* you won't just meet shipping magnates, businessmen and lawyers from the nearby warehouse district of Speicherstadt. The international cuisine includes dishes such as plaice with sautée potatoes; regulars stay longer for a game of cards → p. 71

INSIDER TIP Seaman's pub with TV experience

The *Schellfischposten* is experiencing something of a revival thanks to Ina Müller's TV show 'Ina's Nacht'; but there's always something going on even without cameras → p. 86

INSIDER TIP Haven of peace

HafenCity is one big building site with the sound of drills and the clatter of trucks. But silence reigns in the *Ecumenical Forum* pavilion → p. 46

INSIDER TIP Straight out of Indiana Jones

Snakes, crocodiles, teeming cockroaches and scorpions that glow blue in the dark: Hagenbecks new *Tropical Aquarium* is simply awesome → p. 106

INSIDER TIP Hammonia forever

They are not just beautiful, but age well too. The 'Hamburg bag' from the traditional luggage and bag shop *Klockmann* at the Gänsemarkt (goose market) → p. 78

BEST OF ...

GREAT PLACES FOR FREE
Discover new places and save money

FOR FREE

● *To the bridge!*
It's actually only an office building, but you can go up the *Dockland* free of charge, and from the top you'll have a view of the Elbe like the captain does from his bridge – spectacular (photo) → p. 50

● *Face to face with Antje*
Once the mascot of the local broadcasting company, today the walrus (which is now stuffed) greets visitors young and old to the *Zoologische Sammlung der Universität* (the university's zoological collection) in Grindel – along with tigers, bears and wildebeest. And all that for free ... → p. 106

● *HafenCity at a glance*
The *Infocenter Kesselhaus* not only has a gigantic model of the city and HafenCity, but also lots of interactive information about living in the city – architecture, urban expansion – everything about the future of Hamburg. The centre also runs free tours through HafenCity on weekends → p. 44

● *Organ recitals*
Classical music concerts like this can often cost a lot of money, but in many of Hamburg's churches you don't pay a thing – such as the *Stunde der Kirchenmusik* (hour of church music) that takes place every Wednesday in St Petri, for decades part of the Hamburg music repertoire → p. 35

● *Red bikes*
The environmentally-friendly way: the *Hamburger Stadträder* (city bikes) can be used by anyone and for the first 30 minutes are free – a great service for locals and tourists alike → p. 112

● *Water fountains and Maurice Ravel*
The free water-light concerts in the *Planten un Blomen* park take place every evening in the summer. There is an alternating programme, and the audience is always enthralled when the fountains, colours and music mix. A wonderful way to end the day → p. 38

●●●● Dots in guidebook refer to 'Best of ...' tips

● On the Alster
A real Hamburger is one that goes for a sail at lunchtime. Those with no sailing licence can also rent pedalos and rowing boats from the *Segelschule Pieper* and take to the waters of the beautiful Alster (photo) → p. 104

● Fish market
You've passed the real Hamburg test when you skip the Sunday sleep-in and get up at dawn for a visit to the *Fischmarkt*. Here there are stalls selling fresh fish, seafood, fruit and foodie treats – and the atmosphere is great → p. 50

● Fish with remoulade sauce
It's always really busy at the shipping piers. Buy an extra large fish roll at *Bistro Brücke 10,* then climb the few steps to the observation deck and watch the action from above → p. 38, 64

● Rendezvous with Shahrukh and Rani
Hagenbecks Tierpark is a zoo that is world famous for its herd of elephants. Visitors are welcome to feed them, but only with fruit and vegetables otherwise the pachyderms will get too fat → p. 106

● Panoramic terrace
There's a lot of debate about the HafenCity development, but one thing is certain: the view from the terrace of the *Unileverhaus* right on the water is superb. You can enjoy it with coffee and cake, or an ice cream → p. 47

● On the Reeperbahn at 12.30pm
No visit to Hamburg is complete without a walk along the *Reeperbahn*. If you find the red light district a little too scary on your own, you can book a historical 'prostitute tour'. Extremely insightful and interesting → p. 41

● Among the container giants
Only in Hamburg is there a tour like the *Gigantentour*: by bus to the free port and container docks. It's incredible how high the metal boxes are stacked on the ships → p. 114

ONLY IN

BEST OF ...

● *Undercover*

Rain? In Hamburg you don't need to let a bit of rain get in the way of your shopping. For this is the city of *shopping arcades*. You can just about keep your feet dry all the way from the Jungfernstieg to Mönckebergstraße → p. 77

● *The thicker the better*

Whether the foghorns are sounding on the Elbe or there's a howling gale makes no odds to guests in the *Tower Bar* on the 12th floor of the *Hotel Hafen Hamburg* – they can simply relax and watch from above (photo) → p. 94

● *Stylish and dry*

In *Stilwerk* in the Große Elbstraße you can browse and buy beautiful furniture and home accessories, and at weekends there is even childcare → p. 75

● *Tunnel vision*

The steps lead steeply down, while cars shudder into the deep aboard the adjacent vehicle lift. The walk through the tiled tube of the *old Elbe tunnel* is a very special experience. At the other end you take the lift up and look across at the city's church spires when you emerge → p. 36

● *The world in miniature*

Miniatur-Wunderland in the Speicherstadt really lives up to its name. You could spend hours watching the trains, the traffic, and the aeroplanes taking off and the lights coming on, and marvel at the extraordinary attention to detail → p. 45

● *Quality time with art*

Of course, if the weather's bad the museums are even more appealing. The *Bucerius Kunst Forum* has an exciting programme of exhibitions and is even open on Mondays. There's also a pleasant vegetarian restaurant down by the canal → p. 30

RAIN

RELAX AND CHILL OUT
Take it easy and spoil yourself

● *All steamed up*

A good slap of lather on your back and strong hands massaging away all the tension. At the original Turkish *hamam*, you can forget all about your cares → **p. 35**

● *Where the willows weep*

Almost inaudibly the white Alster steamers ply the canals around the Außenalster lake. The noise of the big city is far away – an ideal place to switch off (photo) → **p. 20**

● *Best foot forward*

At the *Dove Spa* in the Unileverhaus you can enjoy your pampered pedicure with a free view of passers-by thrown in. Afterwards you can always have an ice cream out on the terrace → **p. 47**

● *So romantic ...*

Bathing at the *Holthusen Spa* in Eppendorf is the ultimate in relaxation. Ask them about their romantic candle-lit swims → **p. 114**

● *Relaxing on the Elbe beach*

On the *Strandperle* at Övelgönne you can feel the sand between your toes, slowly sip a drink and enjoy the wonderful view across the Elbe → **p. 51**

● *Park life*

The nicest place to relax in Hamburg is completely free and so comfortable: between spring and autumn you can slump into an old wooden chair on the lawns of the *Alsterpark*. All you need to bring is your sundowner → **p. 105**

● *Wellness in the hotel*

With most of hotel guests out and about during the day, the spas in the better hotels are usually wonderfully peaceful. In many establishments non-residents are welcome, such as at the *Grand Elysée* at the Dammtor → **p. 91**

INTRODUCTION

DISCOVER HAMBURG!

Wind and water – these are the elements which define Hamburg. On a sunny day there's no nicer place to be than the shore of the Außenalster lake: swans and sailing boats and views of luxury villas across the water. While on a stormy day there's nowhere more exciting than the port and its shipping piers, the Landungsbrücken: waves, tug boats and giant container ships. No other city in Germany can boast such growth in its visitor numbers. The only question is: when are you going to come?

There are days on which even die-hard Hanseatics are surprised by their city. On a summer evening they sit with their beer on the beach by the Elbe at Övelgönne, with container ships, harbour ferries and sailing boats passing right in front of them. They take a stroll towards the city centre, past the modern developments of the Elbmeile, gaze across the water from the Dockland office block that juts out over the river and take a detour for a nightcap at the St Pauli beach club. The stroll continues to HafenCity,

Photo: Motor launches in the harbour

where there will probably be another festival going on – jazz or literature. They might hang around for a bit and admire the imposing tinted glass façade of the Elbphilharmonie, which towers over the river. Even now, late in the evening, they're still working here. In the background the new developments of the HafenCity and the illuminated facades of the Speicherstadt (warehouse district) are visible. By this stage these Hamburgers will have looked at each other and said something like: wow, we really do live in a great city!

It's boom time in the 'far north'

The Hanseatics are not alone in this observation. The tourist office recently recorded almost 10 million overnight stays per year, more than ever before. The population of Germany's second-largest city has also been growing for years, soon set to pass the 1.8 million mark. The 'far north' is regarded as the economic powerhouse for an entire region and has recovered from the economic crisis faster than expected. Unemployment is falling and all over the city there is building work going on and new schemes being planned. Hamburg has even become the focus of international attention, featuring on the covers of American glossy magazines. For many the transformation of the city's image has come as something of a surprise. It wasn't always thus: Hamburg used to be the city of *Pfeffersäcke* or moneybags who don't even know how to spell the word 'culture'; the city with the boring brick buildings, the city where it always seems to rain …

The turning point in the city's fortunes focuses on the period just before the fall of the Berlin Wall. Hamburg's mayor at the time was Henning Voscherau and on trips to East Germany he realised one thing: the wall would ultimately fall. In a free Europe the city of Hamburg could develop into a central trading hub between east and west, but for that to happen it first had to be 'woken up from its self-satisfied afternoon nap', as Voscherau put it. So planning went ahead for a fourth Elbe tunnel, the expan-

The port is Hamburg's main asset: both economic and as a tourist attraction

sion of the airport, the Airbus site; schemes for new container terminals such as at Altenwerder were forced through against all opposition. And above all: in secret negotiations the city began buying up land in the harbour area; in secret mainly to avoid speculation. In May 1997, at the Überseeclub on the Alster, Voscherau presented his master plan for the port city to the crème de la crème of the Hanseatic business world: 'returning the inner city to the water can become a reality'. Now this reality has arrived and anyone with the means will buy a loft along the Shanghaiallee or move his law firm into one of the vacant warehouse spaces at the old Wandrahm in the Speicherstadt. The area has a lively primary school, several kindergartens and the HafenCity university is complete. On warm summer evenings, the quays and the cafés are a hive of activity with many cultural events taking place. But that's just one side of the story. Architecture critics rail against prestige projects, by which they mean the numerous boring office blocks. Too many of them still stand empty and most of the rents are far too high. The area lacks a social mix and is dominated by the over 50s. And then there's the

> **Things are happening here – and not just in HafenCity**

Elbphilharmonie, a development increasingly beset by controversy. In conclusion: the development of HafenCity is exciting, but it is far from clear how the whole mega project will pan out.

Its official name is the Free and Hanseatic City of Hamburg. But more than the Hanseatic League, that great maritime trading block of the Middle Ages, it was their freedom that the inhabitants always valued most, and that included freedom from kings, from chancellors and from prelates; freedom from federal state mergers and prime ministers. The long debated merging of the north German federal states will probably continue to be just a vision. As well as attachment to hearth and home there is wanderlust. The tooting of ships in the fog is still heard over the seagull cries in the

neighbourhoods where floods no longer break through the walls. And some have followed the invitation of the ships and set a course for various corners of the world. But at some point they're back: Kehrwiederspitze (come again point) is the name of a street at the start of the old Speicherstadt, where ships once entered and left.

A common prejudice is that Hamburgers are arrogant. But you wouldn't notice it as a tourist walking through the city, whether you came from Germany or abroad. The Hamburgers are more helpful, more open and friendly than you would expect. Many speak excellent English – the relationship to the trading partner at the other side of the Channel has always been a strong one. And continuing in this vain, the real Hamburger is also liberal minded. Whether a life-long punk on Hafenstraße or slick sales promoter, everyone can be just as he or she is. But there is one thing required of everyone: attitude. Here the Hanseatic remains true to his or her mentality – never loses composure and always exercises restraint. Such expectations applied to politicians like Helmut Schmidt just as much as to actors, media people, and captains of industry and every normal citizen of the city. Being over pretentious is frowned upon here.

Enterprising yet liberal-minded and cosmopolitan

For true Hanseatics, actual profit is far more important than outward appearances. It is claimed that Hamburg is now home to more millionaires per capita than any other city in Europe. For many, it seems, business acumen is in their blood. Achieving your goal is not for the faint-hearted. One of the best examples of this is the way Hamburg went about celebrating its 800th anniversary as a port. It was once thought that Emperor Frederick Barbarossa issued a charter for trade on the Elbe on 7 May 1189. In fact this document was uncovered as a forgery as far back as 1907, but such a minor detail was never going stop the Hamburgers celebrating their festival to mark the event – and making a tidy profit putting on the world's biggest port festival.

People enjoy living here and they like to show it. There are around 1000 private charitable foundations active in the city, and whether students or millionaires all delegates to the Hamburg 'donation parliament' have a say in how their money is spent: on the Hamburg Ballet or the Polittbüro theatre and comedy club; on rock events at the Uebel & Gefährlich or on children's theatre. Culture has long been part

THE LOWLANDS? NO WAY!

≈ No hills in Hamburg? Nothing could be further from the truth! The Süllberg in Blankenese is all of 75m/245ft high. And the view from the top can match that of any mountain peak in the Alps ... well, almost. On the Stintfang overlooking the piers it seems like you could be hundreds of feet up – so high and sunny is it up there that there's even a vineyard! You can also view Hamburg from its church spires: St Michael's (Michaeliskirche/Michel), St Peter's (Petrikirche), St James's (Jakobikirche) and St Nicholas (Nikolaikirche). From the viewing platform of the planetarium in the city park you can watch the planes taking off in Fuhlsbüttel. From the top floor of Karstadt's sports shop on Mönckebergstraße you can look straight across the Alster, and the *Highflyer* captive balloon next to the Deichtorhallen will launch you to a height of 150m/490ft *(daily from 10am | tickets 15 euros | weather dependant | tel. 040 30 08 69 69 | www.highflyer-hamburg.de/english/index.html)*.

of everyday life here, even if it slips every now and then. For example many alternative artists have headed for Berlin where the climate is said to be much more supportive. Indeed high culture has always had it much easier in Hamburg than the experimental variety, for instance the city has more than 60 theatres many of which get by with no support. Nowadays lots of new things are happening at the other side of the Elbe, in Wilhelmsburg, Europe's largest inhabited river island. In 2013 it was the venue of the International Garden Show. The International Building Exhibition (the IBA) also took

Green city on the water

place here. They were two major events that helped to transform this once neglected part of the city south of the Elbe. Now it isn't just young families that are attracted to Wilhelmsburg's ultra-modern dwellings, but also day-trippers who come to visit the extensive park with its climbing hall, boating trips and nice restaurants. Hamburg is one of the greenest cities in Germany, with a lake right in the middle. Water from below and water from above – indeed the weather doesn't always play fair. But rain

A lovely spot on the lake: the café terrace at the Jungfernstieg

and fog don't bother the real Hanseatics because there's always compensation in those glorious days when there's a fresh breeze and the air is so clear that you really want to fill your lungs with it.

So why should you visit Hamburg? Very simply, because it is so beautiful here. The Elbe and the Alster offer fantastic panoramic views, and you have a good overview of the city. Even if you just have a weekend it's easy to plan a tour with all the best highlights. If you have more time, go over to the Veddel district. There at the historic shed number 50 is the Harbour Museum. At weekends volunteers work here on the old boats, dredgers and cranes. They will tell you what seafaring used to be like. And then go to the end of the quay (the Hansahöft) and look across: over there is where HafenCity is being created. It is the past, present and future all in one place.

WHAT'S HOT

1 Grey rather than green

Off the fairway Chic golf courses aren't the only places to practise your swing: cross-golfers like doing it on the tops of tower blocks, multi-storey car parks and even ships. One of the most popular venues is the driving range of the 'unlimited possibilities' in the *Golf Lounge (Billwerder Neuer Deich 40 | www.golflounge.de)*. More information about cross-golf in the city can be found at *www.hamburg.cross golf.de* and from the bloggers on *blog.crossgolf.de*. Another online community is *www.wirsindgolf. net,* whose members discuss courses and handicaps.

2 Local music

German-speaking *Krach und Getöse* (noise and din) is the name of the Hamburg music award showcasing local talent. Amongst other events the winners perform at the annual *Dockville Festival*. Up-and-coming German artists also feature at the annual *Lange Nacht Junger Literatur* and *Musik Ham.Lit (photo) (Uebel & Gefährlich and Terrace Hill in the Medienbunker | Feldstr. 66 | www.hamlit.de)*. It was there that the Hamburg band *Nobelpenner (www.myspace.com/nobelpenner)* first unleashed their profound lyrics on the public. Worth listening to if your German is good!

3 Gourmet snacks

Fast food It need not always be a burger. At *Mutterland (Lenhartzstr. 1 | www.mutterland.de) (photo)* there's a choice of delicious open sandwiches. Vegetarian fast food can be enjoyed at *Hin & Veg (Schulterblatt 16 | www.hinundveg.de)*. Even big meat eaters will more than get their fill at *Seitan Burger! Qrito's (Grindelalle 79 | www.qrito.de)* friendly and incredibly fast team will fill your quesadilla or burrito in a blink of an eye.

Gängeviertel

Open-air museum Hamburg's Gängeviertel is probably the most creative and vibrant part of the city. By occupying houses artists and creative types prevented the demolition of historic buildings, now being renovated by a cooperative. Studios and galleries signal a thriving subculture such as at the *Kupferdiebe (Caffamacherreihe 43–49 | www.diekupferdiebe.de)*, where the temporary exhibitions and the open-air gallery are well worth a visit. At the *Jupi Bar (Caffamacherreihe 37–39)* there is a programme of live gigs, readings and the suspiciously cult-like 60-plus dance night called 'Faltenrock' (pleated skirt): young people can only join the party *(every 1st Saturday of the month)* when accompanied by someone who's actually over 60. Information on the alternative art scene in the neighbourhood and tips on walks and guided tours can be found at *http://das-gaengeviertel.info/en.html*

Not off the peg

Design Santa Fu – kreative Zelle, as the label is called, has its products made by prisoners, and here on the Elbe prison outfits with witty prints are all the rage *(www.santa-fu.de)*. *Knit Nights* creates its unique wares not behind bars but with needles: knitting enthusiasts conjure cool clothes and accessories that have absolutely nothing to do with grandpa's socks. They gather at *Mylys (Weidenallee 12 | www.mylys.de)* and their creations *(photo)* are sold on Saturdays *(mid March–Dec)* at the market for fashion and jewellery design in *Unileverhaus (Strandkai 1 | www.derdiesein.de)*. You can find more information on Hanseatic designers at *www.hamburgunddesign.de*.

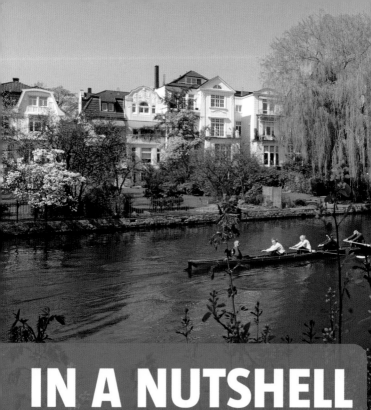

IN A NUTSHELL

BRICKS

As Fritz Schumacher, the head of the city's planning department back in the mid 1920s once put it: 'brick makes constructing new buildings that much easier in the best possible way.' The director of the Art Gallery, Alfred Lichtwark, described his ideal building as follows: 'simple bricks with light mortar joints' with a 'roof of red tiles' and, please, 'no columns, ornament or timber framing'. Brick buildings are a feature of the city and can be found everywhere, from detached houses in Ohlsdorf to housing estates in Barmbek, from the old Speicherstadt warehouse district down by the harbour to HafenCity. Some years ago there was a fierce dispute between proponents of brick and those of glass. Architects such as Hadi Teherani were making the people of Hamburg furious with their new glass palaces. Modern is fine — but in brick please! That's how it was in the past and that's how it should stay. And by the way, the fascinating annual publication brought out by the local literature crowd is called 'The Hamburg Brick' — and there's nothing old fashioned about that!

BUSINESS CARDS

A strange heading, you might think. Who in the era of bluetooth still has a business card? Well, a lot of people in Hamburg.

Moneybags, ships and the Hanseatic people: characteristics and noteworthy features of Hamburg

After all, it isn't just the name that's printed on the card, but it also tells people about where you come from in Hamburg. And that is the all-important question: to the west (good) or east (bad) of the Alster? North (-) or south (+) of the salmon and scampi equator Stresemannstraße/ Olsdorfer Landstraße? New residents of Hamburg often think it doesn't matter whether one lives in Eimsbuettel (-) or Eppendorf (+). After all, the two trendy neighbourhoods adjoin each other. Both have wonderful old buildings, nightmarish rents and chic cafés and bars. But the real Hamburger knows: they are worlds apart!

FLOODING

First of all: had there been no flooding in 1962, Helmut Schmidt – who was Minister for Internal Affairs in Hamburg at the time – would not have been able to demonstrate that he had the makings of a future German Chancellor. When the banks burst in Wilhelmsburg, the decisive action he took saved the lives of thousands of people. The subject has now become more a myth than a fact: the plaques that commemorate the great floods in Övelgönne and in Blankenese tell of a certain pride – 'look at us now; we even survived that'. The subject is, however, deadly serious. Climate experts in Hamburg reckon with a long-term rise in sea level of 30cm. The 103km/64mi long embankment in the city has been or is still in the process of being raised to a height of 9.25m/30ft. The planned dredging of the Elbe shipping lane has come in for a lot of criticism: as the river runs faster the tide will come in faster and with greater force. New developments take account of the flooding threat: in HafenCity all new buildings are constructed on plinths and in emergencies residents can be evacuated via higher-lying streets or bridges. The neighbouring historic Speicherstadt (warehouse district) on the other hand is helplessly exposed to the smallest rise in sea levels – and that's why nobody is actually allowed to live here, at least for now. Of course regardless of any flood danger there have long been enquiries from investors about developing chic lofts and hotels in the area.

GREEN CITY

Hamburg is green: there is the Elbe and the Alster, between them the major parks and green spaces and still relatively tolerable traffic that make life here so agreeable. While Hamburg was named 'Green Capital of Europe' for 2011, the far north still has some way to go in the environmental protection stakes. Between 1990 and 2020 the city wants a 40 per cent reduction in CO_2 emissions, but by 2007 it had only managed 15 per cent. A coal-fired power station has been built in Moorburg and for most Hamburgers waste separation is unheard of. The public transport system is well developed, but expen-

OUT ON THE WATER

You'll be spoiled for choice at the Landungsbrücken piers. The smaller launches chug around the narrow canals in the Speicherstadt warehouse district, the bigger boats can make it across to the container ship terminals. There are numerous services that run from the piers, or from near the Überseebrücke if heading for Baumwall. Most tours cost the same (duration 1 hour). Just as nice as a trip around the harbour is a ● cruise on the Alster. The elegant white boats set out from the Jungfernstieg. You can even get married on board. All sorts of different tours are available, and you might want to look out for family discounts. You can criss-cross the Alster with the *Alster-Kreuz-Fahrt (hourly April– Oct | 1.70 euros per stop, day ticket 12 euros)* which travels from Jungfernstieg to the Winterhude ferry terminal, stopping at nine places where you can hop on and off as you like. The *Fleetfahrt (April–Oct 3x daily, Nov/Dec 1x daily | 2 hours | 20 euros)* takes in the Speicherstadt; or if you'd like an evening tour there's the romantic *Dämmertörn (May–3 Oct daily 8pm | 2 hours | 20 euros | tel. 040 3 57 42 40 | www. alstertouristik.de/English/home.html*

sive, and people find it difficult to understand the complex fare structure of zones and rings. But there's one thing that has really been a resounding success: the funky red city bikes! This is hardly surprising as the first 30 minutes are free, and even non-sporty types are keen to have a ride. The question remains of the city authorities: why don't they apply the same principal to the public transport system?

survived to the present it is the Hanseatic mentality. A Hanseatic merchant embodies many virtues: he is proud of his traditions, is honest and direct, but never short-tempered. A true Hanseatic citizen doesn't look back ('what's done is done ...'), but forward. And this can be seen in the 22,587 new companies registered with Hamburg's Chamber of Commerce in 2010 – more than ever before in the history of the city.

Queen Mary 2 visits St Pauli: the luxury liner off the Landungsbrücken

Buses and trains could be free for the first half hour. Surely this is a brilliant idea and something worthy of a Green Capital.

HANSEATIC LEAGUE

HH – these are the first two letters on the number plates of all cars registered in Hamburg and they stand for 'Hansestadt Hamburg'. Between the 13th and 15th centuries Hamburg belonged to the Hanseatic League, at the time the most powerful city alliance in the world. There is little left now in the city to remind us of those days, unlike in Rostock, Bremen and Lübeck. If there is one legacy that has

HSV OR ST PAULI?

This has always been a crucial issue in Hamburg and one in which football only plays a secondary role. Even kids at the nursery will come to blows over the issue with their buckets and spades, not to mention the fathers and of course the mothers too. Based at Millerntorplatz St Pauli FC still cultivates the myth of being the underdog, but this is changing now, as fans are up in arms about the fancy new stadium complete with VIP area and other trendy facilities. Also the venerable HSV (Hamburg Sports Club), which is the only club to have remained in the *Bundes-*

liga without interruption since its inception, has long been beset by arguments, whether internally in the management or externally due to hooligans. Everyone finds it really annoying that the HSV changes the name of its stadium so regularly that hardly anyone can keep up. The conclusion for a not insignificant group of true football fans in the city is to forsake those clubs and move to Altona 93 – where at least it is still mostly about the game. *www.hsv.de | ticket hotline: tel. 01805 4 78 47 (*); www.fcstpauli.de | ticket hotline: tel. 01805 99 17 19 (*)*

MONEYBAGS

This derogatory term (in German *Pfeffersäcke*) for the enterprising merchants of Hamburg, likely used in connection with any conceivable subject in Hamburg, has a long tradition. It was first used by Denmark's King Christian IV (1577–1649). A quotation from one of his letters about the citizens of Hamburg says it all:

'Arrogant skinflints and moneybags, slimy fishmongers and lazybones ...'

QUEEN MARY & CO

When the 'Queen Mary' comes to town, Hamburgers as well as tourists line the banks of the Elbe by the thousand. They wave and jostle around, there is a special coverage of the event on television, bakers bake bread rolls in the shape of a ship: it's party time on the Elbe. The number of cruise ships arriving in Hamburg increases year on year. 'Cruise days' (when several ships arrive in port at the same time) are regularly organised and provide further delight to the fans. In Altona a brand new cruise terminal has been opened next to the old one. And at some stage there will be further developments in HafenCity — whereby the brightly coloured containers of the Cruise Center, originally meant as a temporary structure, have been a colourful and eye-catching feature for years now.

Red brick gives the Speicherstadt its characteristic appearance

THE CITY BELONGS TO US

For decades, nay centuries, urban planning in Hamburg followed the same pattern. Whether the Speicherstadt or a working-class district, whether an airport or port extension – wherever anything stood in the way of Hanseatic pursuit of profit it was torn down, relocated or built anew without anyone caring very much. But in recent years the citizenry has been getting increasingly vocal in its opposition to certain developments. You might have Gucci ladies from the Elbe suburbs planning sit-ins for the preservation of the Altona Museum, celebrities organising concerts in the Gängeviertel in order to prevent the eviction of the arts scene, and for years now in Altona there has been a battle surrounding the preservation of a disused department store. It will be interesting in the next few years to see what happens to the old the railway land in Altona, which is set to be completely redeveloped, and in the Schanzenviertel, where for years there has been a bitter struggle for the preservation of the *Rote Flora Theatre* community centre. At the same time, the latter district is experiencing a yuppie-style boom that no one had expected to happen so quickly. So it looks like parties are headed for an irreconcilable encounter. *www.rechtaufstadt.net* is one of the websites that summarises the various campaigns taking place in the city.

WILHELMSBURG

There were times when Wilhelmsburg, Europe's largest river island, was off-limits to the fine people of Hamburg. You simply didn't go there – too ugly, too multicultural and anyway: what is one supposed to do there? Today that is all changing; many people want to go, from mayoral candidates in an electoral campaign to people scouting a location for a chic bar. Wilhelmsburg's is still gritty and multicultural and the first impression may be rather off-putting, particularly for tourists who get out at the S-Bahn station. But change is afoot: the International Building Exhibition (IBA) in Wilhelmsburg lasted seven years (2006–13), and it didn't only transform the outward appearance of the district. Much more important than a few smart modern buildings or gardens (which however are really worth seeing) are the changes in attitude that the IBA as well as the International Garden Show 2013 have brought about. For the first time in the history of the city Hamburgers are aware of this district to the south of the Elbe. The oft-cited 'leap across the Elbe' actually seems to have succeeded. There's a wonderful view of the island from the 30m/100ft high terrace of the INSIDER TIP *Energiebunker* (Neuhöfer Str. 7). In the *Café Vju* (Wed–Mon 10am–6pm | tel. 0151 20 51 55 42) they serve coffee and delicious cakes from their own patisserie. *www.igs-hamburg.de/en*

THE PERFECT DAY
Hamburg in 24 hours

08:30am BREAKFAST: THE HANSEATIC WAY

Granted, this tour is demanding and requires a certain amount of exertion. But once you've done it you'll even have locals calling you an insider. The day begins in a dignified manner, just as the Hamburgers like it: classic, elegant, there's no better way to start the day than breakfast in the 'Condi' in the *Hotel Vier Jahreszeiten* → p. 94, whose guests you will also see here *(Mon–Fri from 6.30am, Sat/Sun from 7am)*.

09:30am HAFENCITY ADVENTURE

For those who want to be active: right opposite you can pick up one of the red city bikes and set off to the *Rathaus* → p. 35 (photo left), before continuing via the historic Altstadt to *HafenCity* → p. 42. Alternatively at Jungfernstieg take the U-Bahn line 4 and travel for one stop to the Überseequartier. The most amazing attraction there is the *Unileverhaus* → p. 47; from there continue to the *Elbphilharmonie* → p. 44 (photo middle) whose façade is shooting up just as quickly as the construction costs, somewhere into the stratosphere. Now just continue to the *Landungsbrücken* → p. 38, where you leave your bike and continue by ferry 61 or 62 as far as *Dockland* → p. 50; HVV tickets are valid on the boats. You will pass the Landungsbrücken and the *Fischmarkt*. If the weather's good make sure you head for the sun deck – there's nothing nicer!

01:00pm LUNCH BREAK BY THE ELBE

Now it's time for a midday snack. And since you're in Hamburg why not try some fish. The perfect place is the bistro of *Hummer Pedersen* → p. 74 on the Große Elbstraße. Afterwards continue on foot (approx. 40 min) along the Elbe as far as the captains' settlement of *Övelgönne* → p. 51. At the *Museums-hafen* you can have a cup of coffee on board the museum ship, before taking bus no. 112 to Altona station.

02:30pm IN THE NEIGHBOURHOOD

Since it is now still early afternoon, there's enough time for a nice stroll though the pleasant *Ottensen* → p. 51 with its many shops, restaurants, bars and alternative businesses. Leave the station along the

Get to know the best of Hamburg – the very essence of the city – in a relaxed way and all in a single day

Ottenser Hauptstraße, then you're right in the heart of things, in this melting pot of alternatives and the chic creative scene of advertisers, architects and media companies, who have moved in to the renovated industrial buildings here. The *Zeisehallen* → p. 53 on Friedensallee are always well worth a visit: restaurants, shops and cinemas now occupy the sheds of the old ships' propeller factory.

06:30pm WHEN EVENING COMES ...

How about a strong cheese fondue in the cosy *Schweizweit restaurant* → p. 71? Thus fortified, what next? Nightlife of course! So it's off to the Reeperbahn; from Altona station it's just two S-Bahn stops away (S 1, 3). There's not much more to say about the red-light district of the *Reeperbahn* → p. 41, it's all fairly self-explanatory. And there's certainly no shortage of eating establishments. If the weather's nice, after a break in a bar you should go and have another look at *Park Fiction* → p. 40; if it's raining there's always the bar *20 up* → p. 83 on the 20th floor of the *Empire Riverside* hotel, which is perfect for a nightcap. It provides a breathtaking view over the harbour by night as well.

05:00am EARLY MORNING AT THE FISCHMARKT

Night has now turned into morning – maybe even Sunday morning? If that's the case you might want to continue your itinerary with a visit to the *Fischmarkt* → p. 50 (photo above right). It opens its doors at 5am, and you won't be the only visitors to have made it right through the night. And even if you're not interested in buying crates of bananas or pot plants: the exuberant banter employed by the market characters is pure entertainment. But the hustle and bustle is not for everyone. As an alternative you can nurse your hangover at *Erikas Eck* → p. 70. All night and right through to the morning they serve a choice of bread rolls and strong coffee. Voilà – the 24 hours are up. Anything else?

S-/U-Bahn to the starting point: S 1–3, U 1, 2
Station: Jungfernstieg
HVV day ticket: from 5.80 euros

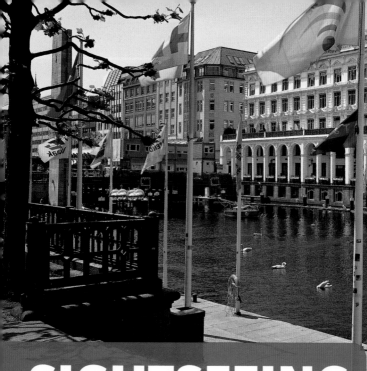

SIGHTSEEING

CITY **WHERE TO START?**
Jungfernstieg **(125 D3)**
(📖 L6): Here you'll have a view over the Binnenalster lake, and there is one chic shop after another. It's only a few steps through the Alster arcades to the Rathausmarkt with the impressive Rathaus (city hall), from where the Mönckebergstraße shopping street leads to the main railway station. Several U- and S-Bahn lines stop at Jungfernstieg station, and there are buses at the Rathausmarkt and several car parks in the area.

Hamburg city centre is compact: whether it's shopping, culture, the excitement of the port or catching your breath in a park – everything is within walking distance.

The most important message to all visitors to Hamburg is: leave the car behind. Apart from a few exceptions, Hamburg's attractions can all be reached by U- and S-Bahn or even by boat. The Hamburg Card *(www.hamburg-tourismus.com)* will provide you with free travel on public transport, or in good weather you can always take a red city bike *(→ p. 112)* and cycle from one destination to the next. The many interesting museums in the centre will entice you to stop; everything is close together.

Photo: Alster arcades on the Binnenalster

A city for all the senses: modern architecture and districts full of atmosphere, interactive museums and art on every corner

From the city hall to HafenCity it's almost half a mile as the crow flies. Between them, amongst other things, lies the old Speicherstadt warehouse district, which is Hamburg's jewel on the River Elbe. It should be a Unesco World Heritage Site, at least that's what many Hamburgers feel and it's a wish that's entirely justified: the fantastic, closed ensemble of warehouses from the late 19th and early 20th centuries in the typical Hamburg red brick style is unique in the world.

If you have just a bit more time then you can experience Hamburg's great diversity in its individual neighbourhoods: Eppendorf, St Georg, Altona, Winterhude, Eimsbüttel and Blankenese were all once villages or small towns independent of Hamburg. All of them have their nice little peculiarities that are worth discovering.

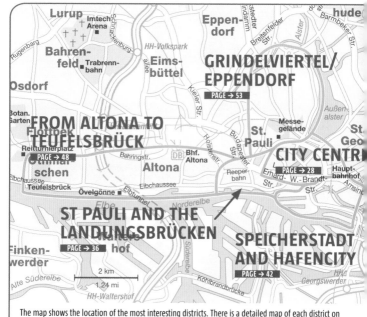

The map shows the location of the most interesting districts. There is a detailed map of each district on which each of the sights described is numbered.

And everywhere there are wonderful pubs, good restaurants, whimsical boutiques, colourful shops, markets, theatres and cinemas.

CITY CENTRE

In the city centre it's mostly about one thing: spending money. There's one shopping arcade after another with everything ranging from luxury boutiques to cheap outlets, department stores to jeans shops and expensive restaurants to simple snack bars.

Amid all this commercialism you should not neglect the cultural side of things. Some of the best museums are situated right here in the heart of the city, and

even if you don't have much time they're still worth a visit. And then of course there's the magnificent Rathaus (city hall), with the following inscription high above the doorway: *Libertatem quam peperere maiores digne studeat servare posteritas*: 'May the freedoms won by their forebears be preserved with dignity by future generations'. A good motto to remember when strolling about town.

■ ALTSTADT (125 D–E5) (*⌀ M7*)
Hamburg's old town is built around the historic Elbe port on the Nikolaifleet canal. However, almost nothing now remains of the original buildings. Almost all medieval structures fell victim to the fire of 1842, or were subsequently demolished. Great mercantile office blocks, the *Kontorhäuser*,

were built in their place. But since the end of the war not as much has changed here as in other parts of Hamburg. Take a stroll along the Altstädterstraße or Burchardstraße. You will still find the cobbler who knows all his customers, a hat maker and Germany's oldest tea shop, the *Teehandlung Ernst Zwack (Kattrepelbrücke 1)*. Along the Altstädter Twiete are the offices of Hamburg's widely read newspaper for the homeless *Hinz & Kunzt. U 3 Mönckebergstraße*

■2 BINNENALSTER
(125 D–E3) (*∅ L–M6*)

The 'binnen' refers to the part of the lake that was 'inside' the city walls and is the very heart of the city. Take a seat at the Jungfernstieg quay and enjoy the view. Right in front of you is where the white Alster steamers cast off, with a few swans swimming around; in the middle of the Binnenalster is the impressive plume of the Alster Fountain – which at Christmas is replaced by a giant illuminated tree. The former millpond, which took on its present form after the Great Fire of 1842, covers an area of around 45 acres. During World War II it was covered over with cardboard dummies to fool enemy bombers. The technically complicated construction of the public transportation system began in 1967 and took over 15 years to complete. Today several underground and suburban railway lines run right underneath the Binnenalster. The most recent line is the U 4 in HafenCity, the first section of which was opened in 2013 complete with large, ultra-modern stations. The line will ultimately continue as far as the Elbbrücken.

■3 BISCHOFSTURM/DOMPLATZ
(125 D–E4) (*∅ M7*)

This is a historically important corner of the city. Archaeologists believe that the remains of the Hammaburg, the first settlement dating from the 9th century, are buried in the vicinity. The stone tower of Archbishop Ezelin Alebrand (1035–43) was unearthed during construction work in 1962. Since its renovation the new *Exhibition Room (Mon–Fri 7am–7pm, Sat 7am–*

MARCO POLO HIGHLIGHTS

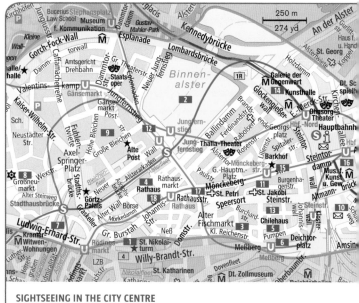

SIGHTSEEING IN THE CITY CENTRE

1 Altstadt	**7** Fleetinsel	**13** Kontorhausviertel
2 Binnenalster	**8** Großneumarkt	**14** Kunsthalle
3 Bischofsturm/Domplatz	**9** Hanseviertel	**15** Mönckebergstraße
4 Bucerius Kunst Forum	**10** Hühnerposten	**16** Museum für Kunst u. Gewerbe
5 Chilehaus	**11** Jakobikirche	**17** Petrikirche
6 Chocoversum	**12** Jungfernstieg	**18** Rathaus

6pm | admission free | Speersort 10) has been established in the basement of a café. The neighbouring cathedral square, the Domplatz, now a green space, was once the site of the Johanneum scholarly institution and, later, the great Catholic cathedral which the citizens irreverently demolished brick by brick between 1804 and 1807. *U 1 Meßberg*

◙ BUCERIUS KUNST FORUM ●
(125 D4) (ØØ L6)

Where would Hamburg be without its generous patrons? Gerd Bucerius, founder of the weekly newspaper 'Die Zeit', was

one of them. In 2002, the Zeit Foundation, which he financed, established an exhibition centre in the former Reichs Bank on Rathausmarkt. The curators have a knack for hosting sophisticated exhibitions that also appeal to a broader public. *Daily 11am–7pm, Thu until 9pm | admission 8 euros | Rathausmarkt 2 | tel. 040 3 60 99 60 | www.buceriuskunstforum.de/en | U 3 Rathaus*

◙ CHILEHAUS (125 E5) (ØØ M7)

On its completion in 1924, the Chilehaus was regarded as one of the 'architectural wonders of the world'. If you stand at the corner beneath the sculpture of the eagle you can easily understand its fascination. Commissioned by the merchant Henry B. Sloman, the architect Fritz Höger used more than 4 million red bricks for its construction. Sloman actually made his fortune importing saltpetre from Chile, hence the name Chilehaus. You can still see that today in the charming animal figures with South American motifs (e.g. in the courtyard portal A, stairwell left). The building was considered a symbol of Hamburg's resurgence after World War I. *Stairwells open only during office hours | U 1 Meßberg*

6 CHOCOVERSUM (125 E5) *(M7)*

Okay, the main purpose behind this attraction might be to sell Hachez chocolate. But what the makers have created around the theme of 'how is chocolate made' is both informative and charming and therefore highly recommended. Warning for those with a sweet tooth: the chocolate is still warm from the mixer – simply delicious. *Daily 10am–6pm | admission including 90 min guided tour 14 euros | Meßberg 1 | www.chocoversum.de/en.html | U 1 Meßberg*

7 FLEETINSEL (124 C4) *(L7)*

A piece of old Hamburg has been preserved along Admiralitätsstraße and its adjacent Fleeten (canals). Today it is particularly popular with art lovers: some of the best galleries in the city are located in the old merchant houses here, renovated by a generous patron. You will also find the wonderful art bookshop of *Sautter + Lackmann*. There's also a handful of good restaurants and in the summer a nice street festival with artistic ambitions. *S 1, 3 Stadthausbrücke*

8 GROSSNEUMARKT
(124 B4) *(L7)*

The 'big new market' (it acquired this name because there was already a smaller 'new market' near the Nicolaikirche) was once the assembly point for Hamburg's militia. Today there are lots of nice pubs on the Großneumarkt; in summer you can eat outside beneath romantic lights. Take a short walk away from the square through the Neustadt – in contrast to the historic old city, this district used to lie outside the city walls. In the Neustadt district you can still see a few restored half-timbered houses and in Peterstraße a complete row of fine baroque buildings has been restored. The scheme is somewhat controversial among conservationists (pseudo-Disneyland) but most people will be happy that a patron took the initiative once again. This time it was Alfred C. Toepfer. *S 1, 3 Stadthausbrücke*

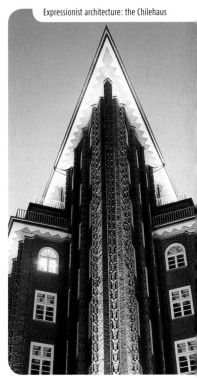

Expressionist architecture: the Chilehaus

The tables of the 'Alex' Alster pavilion at the Jungfernstieg are very inviting

9 HANSEVIERTEL (124 C3) *(Ø L6)*

Built in 1980, the Hanseviertel was the city's first really large shopping centre. The Hamburg architect's firm of GMP (van Gerkan, Marg and Partners) made their international breakthrough with what was at the time a spectacular glass dome building. Poor management plunged the centre into something of a crisis, but there are still a few individual shops here, and most notably the champagne and lobster stand for a luxury snack on Saturday mornings. Shopping arcades have a long tradition in the city: the first one was 'Sillems Bazar', a passageway built in 1845 which was later replaced by the swanky new hotel Hamburger Hof (today also an arcade). The *Colonnaden,* Hamburg's most beautiful old shopping street, was also constructed in the mid 19th century. The prestigious house façades with their magnificent arcades imbue a certain Italian flair – in summer, there is one restaurant terrace after another in the front section. A popular meeting place is *Der Bocksbeutel (daily | Colonnaden 54),* with good wines and friendly people. *S-/U-Bahn Jungfernstieg*

10 HÜHNERPOSTEN (125 F4) *(Ø M7)*

A nice spot for tourists to warm up, surf the internet or read the newspaper, for this is the location of the *Zentralbibliothek (central library: Mon–Sat 11am–7pm | Hühnerposten 1 | tel. 040 42 60 62 15 | www.buecherhallen.de | S-/U-Bahn Hauptbahnhof).* It's all been newly renovated with lots of hi-tech. The two striking bronze figures on the forecourt were created by sculptor Stephan Balkenhol.

11 JAKOBIKIRCHE (125 E4) *(Ø M7)*

The Church of St James is one of the Hanseatic city's five main churches. It was badly damaged during the war but its most valuable possession, the baroque Arp-Schnitger organ with its 60 stops, remained unscathed. There is an organ recital every Thursday at noon. *Mon–Sat 10am–5pm, Oct–March 11am–5pm, tower open at irregular times | Jakobikirchhof 22 | www.jacobus.de/neu/english/index. html | U 3 Mönckebergstraße*

12 JUNGFERNSTIEG (125 D3) *(Ø L6)*

The Hamburgers call this 'the most beautiful shopping street in the world'. That might be a bit of an exaggeration, but the street really is very nice – especially when there's no construction work going on. Unfortunately commerce has completely taken over: in summer there's a never-ending series of street fairs with stalls. What would the writer Heinrich Heine have made of these colourful goings on? He really enjoyed poking fun at the Hanseatic 'moneybags' (merchants) while drinking his coffee in the Alster Pavilion. The ☀ Alsterpavillon (today containing the *Alex café*) is still there today, however not so much a meeting place for intellectuals as for tourists and visitors from the suburbs. Be that as it may, the view from the terrace is still stunning. *S-/U-Bahn Jungfernstieg*

⬛13 KONTORHAUSVIERTEL
(125 E4–5) (*ω M7*)

The Kontorhausviertel was created between the late 19th century and early 20th century. It is the location of such enormous buildings as the *Chilehaus* or the even larger *Sprinkenhof (Burchardstr. 4–6)*. On its completion in 1932 the latter was considered the largest office building in the world. The architects were Fritz Höger and the brothers Hans and Oskar Gerson, and construction took 16 years. Note the net-like pattern on the façade and the gilded terracotta stones; the round stairwell is a masterpiece. The first *Kontorhaus* in Hamburg was actually the old *Dovenhof* on Brandstwiete, it was built by Martin Haller who was already a famous architect was in his own lifetime. The Laeiszhalle, the Hapag Building on Ballindamm and Hamburg's city hall are all by him. The Dovenhof was very modern in its day: there was a paternoster lift, an in-house postal service and the heating costs were charged precisely according to square metreage of space. Even today the building is considered a model. Unfortunately, the badly

damaged building was demolished at the end of the war. *U 1 Steinstraße, Meßberg*

⬛14 KUNSTHALLE ⭐ (125 E3) (*ω M6*)

Hamburgers have an ambivalent relationship to their art. On the one hand they consider culture to be of 'prime importance' to the state, but on the other many don't seem to realise that their Kunsthalle is one of the most important art museums in Germany. Special exhibitions such as the Giacometti in 2013 are packed out of course, but you will hardly see anyone among the wonderful permanent collections even though a visit is always worthwhile. Go and see the old masters – in particular Master Bertram's altarpiece, and marvel at the masterpieces of classical modernism by artists ranging from Max Liebermann to Emil Nolde and Pablo Picasso. In the *Galerie der Gegenwart* – a cuboid building designed by Oswald Mathias Ungers and connected to the Kunsthalle via an underground passageway – you will find works by Gerhard Richter, Jeff Koons and Georg Baselitz. Small-scale special exhibitions are staged in the *Hubertus-Wald-Forum*. You can treat yourself to a break in the *Café Liebermann*. *Tue–Sun 10am–6pm, Thu until 9pm | admission 8.50 euros | Glockengießerwall | tel. 040 4 28 13 12 00 | www.hamburger-kunsthalle.de/index.php/home_en.html | S-/U-Bahn Hauptbahnhof*

⬛15 MÖNCKEBERGSTRASSE
(125 D–E4) (*ω M6–7*)

The elegant curve of this 29m/95ft wide street was cut through the old city between 1908 and 1911. At the same time, the tunnel was dug for the underground. Craftsmen, coachmen and workers were moved out. A few years earlier, cholera had spread through the streets around the Jakobikirche. *Kontorhäuser*, grand office buildings, were constructed and

Where local policy is decided: chamber of the Hamburg Parliament in the city hall

at the top end of Spitalerstraße, Fritz Schumacher designed the Mönckeberg Fountain to 'promote city living'. Today Mönckebergstraße is always busy, not to say packed. Previously, it was characterised mainly by cheap shops, sausage stands and men loitering with beer cans in their hands. The creation of the Europa-Passage brought an upswing, but it has to be said that the sausages from the two stands opposite each other near C&A still taste great. Also, drop by the *Kulturcafé* at the Mönckeberg Fountain. On the outside it's just a Starbucks, but inside there's information about the Elbphilharmonie. You can also purchase concert tickets (they still perform in the Laeiszhalle) or book a tour of the enormous Elbphilharmonie building site *(www.elbphilharmonie.de/ kulturcafe)*. U 3 Mönckebergstraße

16 MUSEUM FÜR KUNST UND GEWERBE (125 F4) *(∅ N6)*

This museum of arts and crafts is a must for any visitor to Hamburg interested in culture. The enormous building near the

railway station has been undergoing renovations for years now. Much has been completed, including the wonderful design department with original canteen of the weekly magazine 'Der Spiegel' as its centrepiece. One can only admire for the vision of the first museum director, Justus Brinckmann: in 1900 he purchased a complete art nouveau room in Paris. The museum is also renowned for its East Asia section; for years now the authentic Japanese tea ceremony held in the Japanese teahouse has been an institution. Check the times before you go. The temporary exhibitions are always interesting and afterwards you can enjoy a delicious salad in the pleasant museum café, the *Destille*. *Tue–Sun 10am–6pm, Wed/ Thu until 9pm | admission 10 euros | Steintorplatz | tel. 040 4 28 13 48 80 | www.mkg-hamburg.de/en | S-/U-Bahn Hauptbahnhof*

17 PETRIKIRCHE (125 D4) *(∅ M7)*

Without any feeling for the injured pride of the residents of Hamburg, Napoleon's soldiers stabled their horses in this massive brick church, Hamburg's oldest parish church dating from 1195. And, as if that were not enough, shortly before Christmas 1813, the French commander ordered the citizens to stock up on provisions for the coming months. Those who could not do so were threatened with expulsion. Thousands of these poorest of the poor spent a night full of fear and cold in the Petrikirche before being driven out of the city through the Millerntor gate on 25 December. A painting in the church now commemorates the event. Every Wednesday at 5.15pm you can listen to organ music during the popular ● *Stunde der Kirchenmusik (hour of church music; admission free). Mon–Fri 10am–6.30pm, Sat 10am–5pm, Sun 9am–8pm | Mönckebergstraße | www.sankt-petri.de | U 3 Rathaus*

18 RATHAUS ⭐ (125 D4) (*𝄕 M6*)

It's well worth taking a tour of the town hall: there's gold and splendour wherever you look, such as in the large Emperor's Hall, so called because it was here, on 19 June 1895 that Kaiser Wilhelm II celebrated the opening of the Kiel Canal. The great and the good of Hamburg still gather here every February, as they have done ever since 1356 to celebrate the Matthias feast along with 'representatives of those powers friendly towards Hamburg'.

During the Great Fire of 1842, the old town hall near the Trost Bridge was blown up in the hope that this would help contain the blaze and prevent things getting worse. Subsequently there were decades of squabbles and discussions about a replacement building. It was not until 1880, when the architect Martin Haller established the 'Town Hall Builders' Society', that there was a breakthrough. The construction presented a big technical challenge. It was necessary to drive 4,000 pylons into the muddy, marshy ground near the Alster. Today, they still support the 111m/364ft wide and 70m/230ft long construction with its 112m/367ft high central tower. Luckily, the city hall suffered only slight damage in World War II and today it is regarded as one of Germany's most important historicist style buildings. The restaurant in the rooms of the former town hall cellar is called *Parlament. Daily Mon–Fri 7am–7pm, often also until 9pm, Sat 10am–6pm, Sun 10am–5pm | guided tours (approx. 45 min) every half hour Mon–Fri 10am–3pm, Sat 10am–5pm, Sun*

RELAX & ENJOY

If you are suffering from a hangover or the weather has taken a turn for the worse then it's off to ● *Hamam Hafen Hamburg* (124 A5) (*𝄕 K7*) *(Mon–Sat 10am–10pm, Sun until 9pm | book in advance | from 30 euros | Seewartenstr. 10 | tel. 040 3 11 08 39 90 | www. hamam-hamburg.de/en/en-das-hamam. html | S-/U-Bahn Landungsbrücken).* Located in a former hospital you can start by sweating it out on one of the marble benches before having a massage and finishing – wrapped up in towels and wearing a bathrobe – by drinking tea reclined on the comfortable cushions in the relaxation room. There are masseuses for the women. If this one is too busy for you, ask about the smaller one in the Karoviertel district: this was where the owners of the business, the Costur family, opened the first of their hamams.

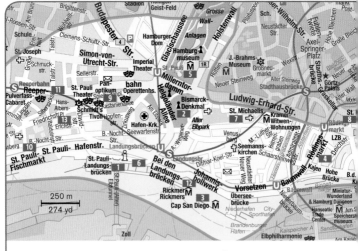

SIGHTSEEING IN ST PAULI AND THE LANDUNGSBRÜCKEN

1. Alter Elbtunnel
2. Bismarck Denkmal
3. Cap San Diego
4. Deichstraße
5. Hamburgmuseum
6. Landungsbrücken
7. Michaeliskirche
8. Nikolaikirchturm
9. Panoptikum
10. Park Fiction
11. Reeperbahn
12. Rickmer Rickmers
13. St Pauli Museum

10am–4pm, except when the council is in session | tickets 4 euros | Rathausmarkt 1 | tel. (recorded message) 040 4 28 31 24 70 | tel. (for groups) 040 4 28 31 20 64 | english. hamburg.de | U 3 Rathaus

ST PAULI AND THE LANDUNGS- BRÜCKEN

It's at the Landungsbrücken piers that the heart of Hamburg's harbour beats. Enjoy the hustle and bustle on the water. Take a walk through the old Elbe Tunnel and enjoy the view back over the city's skyline from Steinwerder. Sensational!

A harbour cruise is a must for everyone – as is a visit to the Hamburg Museum and, of course, you simply have to climb Hamburg's landmark, the tower of the Michaeliskirche (St Michael's Church) where you might even hear the lone trumpeter playing a hymn tune. And then it's off to the Reeperbahn in the evening.

1 ALTER ELBTUNNEL ●
(136 A–B5) (*∅ K7*)

It rattles and shakes and is a real adventure: a descent with the car lift down (24m/ 79ft) to below the level of the Elbe. When the old Elbe tunnel was built in 1911, it was an international sensation. It is 426,5m/ 1,400ft long and originally served the harbour workers on their way to work. The dome on the shipping piers was modelled on the Pantheon in Rome. The tunnel is closed to cars at weekends. *Pedestrians and cyclists round the clock and free, cars only Mon–Fri 5.30am–8pm | 2 euros | S-/ U-Bahn Landungsbrücken*

■ BISMARCK DENKMAL ☆
(136 B5) (*ʘ K7*)

This is the largest memorial in Hamburg; the figure alone is 15m/49ft high. It was unveiled in 1906 but was never popular and Rolf Liebermann, the former opera director, thought it 'an unparalleled monstrosity'. Even today, you won't find many residents of Hamburg here, in spite of the magnificent view of the harbour. The statue of Kaiser Wilhem I experienced a similar fate to that of the derided figure of the chancellor. The equestrian statue dating from 1889 was actually planned for the Rathausmarkt but in 1930 it was moved to where it stands today, on the ramparts, just as resolutely ignored as good old Bismarck. *S-/U-Bahn Landungsbrücken*

■ CAP SAN DIEGO (136 B6) (*ʘ L7*)

This white, streamlined former cargo vessel is moored at the Überseebrücke, where the cruise ships once berthed. Launched in 1961 as the last of a series of six ships, 'Cap San Diego' is the world's largest seaworthy civilian museum ship. Visitors can access virtually all areas of the vessel and it's even possible to take a cabin for the night *(76–95 euros). Daily 10am–6pm | admission 6 euros | Überseebrücke | tel. 040 36 42 09 | www.capsandiego.de | S-/U-Bahn Landungsbrücken*

■ DEICHSTRASSE (126 C5) (*ʘ L7*)

'Fire! Fire on Diekstraat!' This was the cry of the night watchman at one o'clock in the morning of 5 May 1842. What happened over the next three days had a greater impact on Hamburg's appearance

Maritime history at your fingertips: the schooner 'Rickmer Rickmers' and freighter 'Cap San Diego'

than all the destruction of World War II. The Great Fire reduced historic Hamburg to rubble, and one-third of the population was made homeless. Under the leadership of Alexis de Chateauneuf a virtually new city was created: the 'Venice of the North' with the Alster arcades and the Rathausmarkt. Today Deichstraße looks (almost) like it did in 1842, largely thanks to the 'Save Deichstraße' Committee. You can walk along the narrow passageways down to the canals and have a meal there on the jetty. At low tide this is not quite so pleasant – the sludge stinks! *U 3 Rödingsmarkt*

LOW BUDGET

▶ A tour of the Elbe with the Hadag harbour ferries is inexpensive: line 62 takes you from the Landungsbrücken piers to Finkenwerder, where you can change to 64 for Teufelsbrück. From there you can take a bus back to the city centre. A group day ticket (from 9am) costs just 10.40 euros for 5 persons.

▶ ● The water-light concerts – illuminated fountains and cascades with musical accompaniment – are both romantic and free. They take place at the lake in *Planten un Blomen* **(124 B1)** *(øɒ L5)* *(May–Aug daily 10pm, Sept 9pm)*.

▶ You can see Hamburg as it used to be for 2 euros if you visit the *Kramer Witwenwohnung* (almshouse for widows of the Guild of Shopkeepers) near the Michel **(124 B5)** *(øɒ L7)* *(Tue–Sun 10am–5pm, in winter Sat/ Sun only | Krayenkamp 10)*

■5 ■ HAMBURGMUSEUM
(124 A4) *(øɒ K6)*

The façade itself is pure splendour and the interior of the museum, which was planned by Fritz Schumacher and inaugurated in 1922, impresses with its magnificent staircases and halls. Let yourself be transported back to medieval times or to the Great Fire of 1842. From the bridge of the steamship 'Werner' you can observe Hamburg's harbour the way it was in 1938; you can track down the 'moneybags' in their original offices; or guide a model ship up through a lock. In a nutshell: here you can find everything relating to the history of Hamburg. There is even a miniature railway (rides, four times daily). If you grow tired visit the *Café Fees* in the covered courtyard. *Tue–Sat 10am–5pm, Sun 10am–6pm | admission 8 euros | Holstenwall 24 | tel. 040 42 81 32 23 80 | www.hamburgmuseum.de | U 3 St Pauli*

■6 ■ LANDUNGSBRÜCKEN ★
(136 A–B 5–6) *(øɒ K7)*

If statistics are to be believed, the Landungsbrücken piers are – after the Brandenburg Gate in Berlin – Germany's second most visited tourist attraction. The pontoon installation was constructed between 1904–1910 and indeed, there is always nonstop bustle on the water with is the continuous coming-and-going of the harbour ferries, interspersed by the catamaran to Helgoland or one of the two paddle steamers. The bridges are numbered to help with orientation. For example, the Hadag line ferry 62 is stationed at pier 3. Don't be put off by the commotion made by captains promoting their harbour tours, the harried commuters and daytrippers with their bikes. ● Buy a fish sandwich (pier 10), find a place on the steps and watch the action from above. It's never quiet here, even later on when the people crowd into the new *Hard Rock*

Café or the new *Blockhaus*. *S-/U-Bahn Landungsbrücken*

7 MICHAELISKIRCHE ★
(124 B4–5) (*∅ L7*)

The Michaeliskirche (St Michael's Church) – is the city's most important landmark. No other church is held in such esteem by the people of Hamburg. If the church needs attention, they rally and make donations. The present magnificent baroque building was designed by the architects Johann Leonard Prey and Ernst Georg Sonnin and was completed in 1786. After a fire completely destroyed the church in July 1906, the Senate immediately decided to reconstruct it on the same site, using the original plans. You should not leave Hamburg without visiting 'Michel'. Wonderful concerts are held here, for example during the Bach Weeks every autumn, and the Christmas concerts and services are very atmospheric when the white wood of the balustrades with its gold ornamentation is illuminated only by candlelight. The tower is 132m/433ft high, and 452 steps lead to the top (there is also a lift). A tip is the INSIDERTIP *Nachtmichel (night Michel; start your climb to the right of the main entrance | usually daily from 7.30pm, irregular times in winter | admission 9.90 euros | tel. 040 28 51 57 91 | www. nachtmichel.de):* from the deck, which is open until late, you can enjoy the sea of lights across Hamburg. Included in the price is a drink in the small, lounge-like tower room complete with corner seating and heaters. You can also visit the crypt, which was only opened a few years ago. Hamburg's former musical director Philipp Emanuel Bach (1714–88) lies buried here. The second son of Johann Sebastian Bach succeeded Georg Philipp Telemann in the post in 1767. *Daily Nov–April 10am–5.30pm, May–Oct 9am–7.30pm (visits are not possible during services), tower chorale*

Distinctive towers: Hotel Hafen Hamburg and the Michaeliskirche

Mon–Sat 10am and 9pm, Sun noon | Englische Planke 1a | tel. 040 37 67 80 | www.st-michaelis.de | express bus 37 Michaeliskirche

8 NIKOLAIKIRCHTURM
(125 D5) (*∅ L7*)

The 147m/182ft high tower was the only section of the Church of St Nicholas to survive the bombings of World War II, and it is now a memorial. The former main church was not very old at the time of its destruction, having been rebuilt in the style of a medieval Gothic cathedral after the Great Fire. The plans for that were drawn up by Gottfried Semper, the famous builder of the Semper Opera House in Dresden who came from Hamburg and earned his first laurels as a member of the 'Technical Commission'. Included in the entrance fee of 3.70 euros for the war documentation centre is the ticket for the glass lift up the tower. At a height of 76m/ 249ft the viewing platform provides a fantastic panoramic view, which can be compared to the INSIDER TIP poignant photographs of the destroyed city. *May– Sept daily 10am–8pm, Oct–April until 5pm | www.mahnmal-st-nikolai.de | U 3 Rödingsmarkt*

9 PANOPTIKUM (136 A5) *(ɰ K7)*

Things are continually changing along the Reeperbahn – but the Panoptikum is still there, in the same spot it has occupied since 1879 and is now in the fourth generation and run by the great-grandson of the founder. 120 wax figures await you, including Harry Potter alias Daniel Radcliffe, style guru Karl Lagerfeld and Albert Einstein. *Mon–Fri 11am–9pm, Sat 11am–midnight, Sun 10am–9pm, closed approx. mid Jan*

to mid Feb | admission 5.50 euros | Spiel- budenplatz 3 | tel. 040 31 03 17 | www. panoptikum.de | S 1, 3 Reeperbahn*

10 INSIDER TIP PARK FICTION (136 A5) *(ɰ J7)*

It is an exciting place, this rather offbeat little park at the edge of St Pauli, which enjoys a fantastic view of the harbour. It was born out of a local neighbourhood action group that managed to prevail against the developers. Now, you can sip a beer or latte under artificial palm trees among punks, market researchers and children playing ball. Right next door is the once embattled port road, below at the Fischmarkt Hamburg's cult nightclub *Golden Pudel,* and right opposite the floating docks of Blohm + Voss. All of which gives the area a really special atmosphere. *Corner Antonistr./Pinnasberg | park-fiction. net/category/english | S 1, 3 Reeperbahn*

Colourful, loud and always busy: Spielbudenplatz on the Reeperbahn

11 REEPERBAHN ●
(136 A–B5) (*Ø J–K7*)

Come on, admit it: you really are interested in the Reeperbahn, where else can you so openly come into contact with a red-light district? Sex for money still plays an important role on Hamburg's so-called 'sin mile'. There are several thousand officially registered prostitutes and a large number who are not. During the day, the area is quite dreary but it becomes more colourful at night with the lights and neon signs. Background information is provided by the INSIDERTIP 'Historical Whore Tour' *(Thu–Sat 8pm, advance booking required, German speakers only | minimum age 18 | Meeting point Davidwache | 29.50 euros | tel. 01805 12 52 25 (*) | www.hurentour.de)*. Don't get the wrong idea: the ladies are trained guides and absolutely respectable. Of course, they tell it like it is. But the district is changing. At the once legendary

address of Reeperbahn Nr. 1 there now stands the *Tanzenden Türme* (dancing towers), two steel and glass office blocks. There are also plans for new schemes at Spielbudenplatz to the south. The iconic Esso petrol station will have to give way to the chic new neighbourhood as will old well-established music clubs such as the *Molotow*. Those looking for that original St Pauli will find it in the side streets around Hans-Albers-Platz and Hamburger Berg street. There are many welcoming pubs, where you can talk and dance the night away. *S 1, 3 Reeperbahn*

12 RICKMER RICKMERS
(124 A6) (*Ø K7*)

You can get a vivid idea of how hard a sailor's life was on Hamburg's first museum ship. It's pretty claustrophobic in a sailor's bunk, and the cook had to be something of an acrobat in the galley. Since 1987, the sleek, green sailing schooner has been moored in the Landungsbrücken at pier 1. Mail a postcard from here; the ship is after all an INSIDERTIP official marine post office. *Daily 10am–6pm | admission 4 euros | Landungsbrücken | tel. 040 3 19 59 59 | www.rickmer-rickmers.de | S-/U-Bahn Landungsbrücken*

13 ST PAULI MUSEUM
(136 A5) (*Ø K7*)

The St Pauli veteran and photographer Günter Zint campaigned for years if not decades for a Saint Pauli Museum. In 2010 his dream finally came true. Of course not everything on display in the well designed rooms is suitable for youngsters. Also part of the collection is the legacy of neighbourhood painter Erwin Ross. Conclusion when leaving: those were the days! *Tue/Wed 11am–7pm, Thu–Sat 11am–10pm, Sun 11am–6pm | admission 5 euros | Davidstraße 17 | www.st-pauli-museum.com | S 1, 3 Reeperbahn*

SPEICHER-STADT AND HAFENCITY

The way the people of Hamburg have produced an entire district from scratch – wrested it from the Elbe – is astonishing. Only a few years ago, this was the site of the free port; sheds and cranes stood where the first tenants of this area now look down on the Elbe from their loft apartments.

There were similarly radical developments here once before: in order to make way for the warehouses of the ★ *Speicherstadt* (warehouse district) at the end of the 19th century thousands of people were forced to leave their homes. Today the amazing ensemble of brick buildings is the jewel of the Hanseatic city. A worthwhile tip is to explore on foot and take a look at the inner courtyards at Holländische Brook and Alte Wandrahm. You can also explore HafenCity on foot. Get off at the Baumwall U-Bahn station (U3). From there it's just a few minutes to the Elbphilharmonie, the Kaiserkai and the Sandtorpark. Take a stroll along the quaysides and ask yourself the question: would you like to live here? A few thousand Hamburgers have already done so. There's a school, restaurants, and new shops open almost daily. Everything here is developing at lightning speed – wherever there's an empty building site there'll be a finished office block a few months later. Sometimes development is too rapid, with tenants and buyers unable to keep up. This is most evident in the Überseequartier, the planned business centre of HafenCity. Rarely is it very busy here: there are a few nice shops, cafés and restaurants, even a modest weekly market, but everything seems a bit cold and lifeless – beginning with the U-Bahn station (U4), whose interior is so grand that it could have been built for the centre of New York. But such a project does involve delusions of grandeur ... If you walk through HafenCity, which you

Once fruit and vegetables, now art and photography: the Deichtorhallen

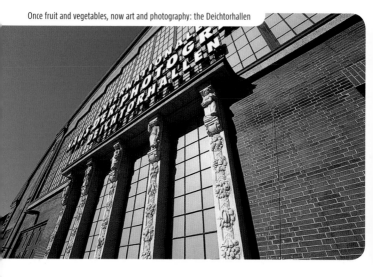

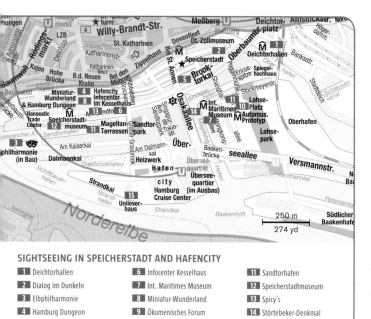

SIGHTSEEING IN SPEICHERSTADT AND HAFENCITY

1. Deichtorhallen
2. Dialog im Dunkeln
3. Elbphilharmonie
4. Hamburg Dungeon
5. HHLA-Zentrale
6. Infocenter Kesselhaus
7. Int. Maritimes Museum
8. Miniatur-Wunderland
9. Ökumenisches Forum
10. Prototyp
11. Sandtorhafen
12. Speicherstadtmuseum
13. Spicy's
14. Störtebeker-Denkmal
15. Unileverhaus

can do very easily despite the many building sites, make sure you take a jacket with you: here on the banks of the Elbe there's often a stiff breeze. *www.hafencity.com/en/ueberseequartier.html | U 4 Überseequartier*

■ DEICHTORHALLEN
(125 F5) (*ω M7*)

This is where the market women from the surrounding area used to sell their wares, keeping their vegetables fresh in underground cellars. The Südhalle (south hall) is now the *Haus der Fotografie* and often mounts exhibitions from the collection of F. C. Gundlach. Opposite, in the Nordhalle (north hall), are displays of contemporary art. The halls are just a 10-minute walk from the main station and on the way you'll pass some galleries, the Kunstverein (art society) and the Academy of Arts, eve-

rything looking a bit inhospitable amid the roaring traffic, but often well worth closer inspection. The launch pad for the *Highflyer* (→ p. 14) is also here. The restaurant for the Deichtorhallen, *Fillet of Soul (daily | tel. 040 70 70 58 00 | Moderate)*, is regarded as one of the city's trendy meeting places. *Tue–Sun 11am–6pm | admission 9 euros | Deichtorstr. 1–2 | www.deichtorhallen.de | U 1 Steinstraße*

■ DIALOG IM DUNKELN
(125 E5) (*ω M7*)

The 'Dialogue in the Dark' exhibition allows you to experience the world of the blind and partially sighted – you will be escorted through total darkness by guides who are themselves blind or partially sighted – an enlightening experience. If you're not alone (one person can always be accommodated) you should definitely sign up in advance for a 60 or 90 minute tour. *Tue–Fri 9am–5pm, Sat 10am–8pm, Sun 10am–7pm | tickets 19 euros | Alter Wandrahm 4 | tel. 040 3 09 63 40 | www. dialog-im-dunkeln.de | U 1 Meßberg*

▣ ELBPHILHARMONIE
(124 C6) (*ᗰ L7*)

The Elbphilharmonie grows and grows – just like its enormous cost. For many critics this multi-million pound project is a byword for the whole of HafenCity: far too expensive, far too elite. And when as a tourist you stand on the heavily built up Kaiserkai and look up, then one can understand the fear of megalomania. Who is going to pay for it all, and where are all the thousands of well-to-do concert-goers going to come from every evening? Information about the controversial Elbphilharmonie project is available from the small pavilion on the *Magellan-Terrassen (Tue–Fri at varying times, information boards always accessible).* The INSIDER TIP▶ building site tours, while still possible, are really exciting and take place at weekends. You'll need to book well in advance, online at *www. elbphilharmonie.de* or in the *Kulturcafé* on Mönckebergstraße (→ p. 34). You can also book a group tour *(from age 14, 5 euros per person). HafenCity, Magellan-Terrassen | bus 111 Magellan-Terrassen*

▣ HAMBURG DUNGEON
(124 C6) (*ᗰ L7*)

This is a kind of modern ghost train devoted to the history of Hamburg: from floods and fire to the cholera epidemic and an execution – there's lots of really scary stuff that's definitely not for children under 10 even though the amateur actors sometimes make the performance unintentionally more comical than frightening. *Daily 10am–5pm | admission 23 euros | Kehrwieder 2 | tel. 040 36 00 55 20 | www.*

thedungeons.com/hamburg/en | metro bus 6 Auf dem Sande

▣ HHLA-ZENTRALE (125 E5) (*ᗰ M7*)

Towers, battlements, oriel windows: the building is more reminiscent of a fairy-tale castle than a company headquarters. This is the home of HHLA, the Hamburg Harbour and Logistics Company. The Speicherstadt, Altenwerder container harbour, Burchardkai and many other developments belonged to this organisation which was founded by the city in 1885. When the Hamburg Senate briefly considered selling off this Hamburg institution to the Deutsche Bahn, there was a public outcry. If you ask the porter nicely he might let you in to see the covered courtyard. *St Annen 11 | metro bus 6 St Annen*

▣ INFOCENTER KESSELHAUS ●
(125 D6) (*ᗰ L7*)

This is an ideal starting point for a tour through the old Speicherstadt and the new HafenCity, complete with café and lots of interactive stuff on the computer screens. The old power station that once served the Speicherstadt also has an 8 × 4m model of the city. Every Saturday at around 3pm free tours head from here through the real HafenCity. *Tue–Sun 10am–6pm | Am Sandtorkai 30 | tel. 040 36 90 17 99 | www.hafencity.com/en/ home.html*

Over a period of seven weekends in the summer, the square in front of the Infocenter is transformed into an open-air stage where the INSIDER TIP▶ *Hamburger 'Jedermann'* (Everyman) is performed. Death arrives by rowing boat, and Jedermann is a typical Hamburg money-bags (merchant): a superb production. *Tickets 18–52 euros | tel. 040 3 69 62 37 | www.hamburger-jedermann.de | metro bus 6 Auf dem Sande*

7 INTERNATIONALES MARITIMES MUSEUM (125 E6) (*M7*)

Built in1879, the Kaispeicher B warehouse at the Magdeburger Hafen harbour is one of the oldest buildings in the Speicherstadt. You simply must have a look at the magnificently restored building. The extensive private collection of the former head of

immhh.de/?lang=en | bus 111 Osakaallee, Überseeallee

8 MINIATUR-WUNDERLAND ★ ● (124 C6) (*L7*)

A model railway that enjoys superlative after superlative, and rightly so. There is only one way to describe what the Braun

Attention to detail: Hamburg city centre at Miniatur-Wunderland

the Springer publishing company Peter Tamm is on display. He started collecting model ships when he was a young boy and assembled tens of thousands over the following decades, together with enormous oil paintings, uniforms, submarines and other items that make maritime enthusiasts happy. You can then relax at the *Meerwein restaurant (closed Sat/Sun | tel. 040 30 08 78 88 | Moderate)*. *Tue–Sun 10am–6pm, Thu until 8pm | admission 12 euros | Koreastr. 1 | www.*

brothers, together with their father and staff, have created in the Speicherstadt: a great experience for the whole family. The numbers are impressive: several hundred thousand figures, more than 10km/ 6mi of track, tens of thousands of wagons, vehicles, etc. It is the largest model railway in the world, operated by 64 computers – and the enthusiasm of the team. The Swiss Alps alone extend over three floors; you can see the Norwegian fjords and a gigantic airport. Since the opening in 2001 there have been over 10 million visitors, more than to any other attraction in Hamburg. The best time to visit is early evening; you can INSIDER TIP book tickets in advance on the website and avoid the queues. And another tip: treat yourself to a tour behind the scenes. *Mon and Wed–Fri 9.30am–6pm, Tue 9.30am–9pm, Sat/Sun 8.30am–9pm (often open longer) | admission 12 euros | Kehrwieder 2 | tel. 040 3 00 68 00 | www.miniatur-wunderland.com | metro bus 6 Auf dem Sande*

9 INSIDER TIP ÖKUMENISCHES FORUM HAFENCITY
(125 D6) (*∅ M7–8*)

Hafencity is dominated by commerce, shops and trendy places to go – the *Ökumenische Forum* (Ecumenical Forum) is intended to provide something of a counterpoint. Almost twenty Christian churches have joined forces to offer a broad spectrum of activities: regular prayers in the attractive chapel *(Mon, Wed, 1pm–1.15pm, Tue, Thu 6pm–6.15pm)*, lectures, music, discussions, and in the attached ☺ *Weltcafé Elbfaire (Mon–Fri 11am–7pm)* snacks and drinks from fair trade products. Note the beautiful curved brick façade with the bell at the top, which always rings before prayers. *Open daily, midday prayers usually at 1 o'clock | Shanghaiallee 12 | www.oekumenisches-forum-hafencity.de | bus 111 Shanghaiallee*

10 PROTOTYP
(125 E6) (*∅ M7*)

A museum for streamlined racing cars from the last 100 years, innovative sports cars, and elegant vintage specimens: this is not only where boyhood dreams become reality; cars also appeal to women – especially the beautiful ones! The racetrack simulator with an old Porsche convertible is great fun. *Tue–Sun 10am–6pm | admission 9 euros | Shanghaiallee 7 | www.*

prototyp-hamburg.de/new/frame.php?page=00&lang=3 | bus 111 Shanghaiallee

11 SANDTORHAFEN (124 C6) (*∅ L7*)

In good weather a pleasant place to go in HafenCity: a few lovely old ships and some sleek pontoons that are real technological marvels (underwater storerooms, swivelling, etc.). The Hamburg Maritime Foundation has invested a lot of time and effort into the project, mostly on a voluntary basis. Call by the harbourmaster's pavilion, which is usually open, where they will gladly answer any questions. The INSIDER TIP historical photos on the railings leading up to the Sandtorkai are really interesting: take a look and compare with the scenes today! *Open 24 hours a day | free admission | metro bus 6 | bus 111 Am Sandtorkai*

12 SPEICHERSTADTMUSEUM
(124 C6) (*∅ L7*)

There was a Speicherstadtmuseum well before HafenCity had even been thought of. And indeed there's hardly a nicer attraction in Hamburg than this lovingly run museum with its moderate prices. It's a must for anybody interested in ships and harbours and history. *April–Oct Mon–Fri 10am–5pm, Sat/Sun until 6pm, Nov–March Tue–Sun 10am–5pm | admission 3.60 euros | Am Sandtorkai 36 | www.speicherstadtmuseum.de/start/start_engl.html | metro bus 6 Auf dem Sande*

13 SPICY'S (124 C6) (*∅ L7*)

Viola Vierk is a Speicherstadt enthusiast. There wasn't much going on here when she first opened her spice museum in 1993, but today it's an institution. You can smell and taste or participate in offbeat walking. *Tue–Sun (July–Oct daily) 10am–5pm | admission 3.50 euros | Am Sandtorkai 32 | tel. 040 36 79 89 | www.spicys.de | metro bus 6 Auf dem Sande*

14 STÖRTEBEKER-DENKMAL
(125 E6) (*M M6*)

It is said that shortly before his death, the famous pirate Klaus Störtebeker made a deal with his executioner: that all the upper floors. The architectural work of art has state-of-the art technology and everything is vibrant, ergonomic and bright. The unobstructed views of the Elbe from the ~ canteen terrace cannot be beaten,

Award-winning office architecture: Unileverhaus in HafenCity

fellow condemned he could walk past – headless – should be set free. Many legends have grown up around the man who wrought havoc on the Elbe and in the Baltic in the 14th century. The large monument shows him in shackles. *Osakaallee (near Busanbrücke) | bus 111 Osakaallee, Überseeallee*

15 UNILEVERHAUS ★ ●
(136 D6) (*M L8*)

You're standing in front of the best office building in the world – at least it was officially confirmed as such by a jury of architects in 2009. Tourists can visit the atrium; the offices themselves are on the though as a rule the canteen itself can only by used by people who work here, of whom there are more than 1,200, except for during events such as the Elbe jazz festival. But the café with its sun loungers is open to all and it's a great place to relax and enjoy. The building also houses a Unilever shop and the trendy ● *Dove Spa (Mon–Fri 10am–8pm, Sat 11am–7pm | tel. 040 34 93 13 55 | www.dovespa.de)*. Next door is the *Marco Polo Tower*, with ultra-expensive apartments that cost many thousands of euros per square metre – but they say the view's worth it. The car park is open for visitors in the evening. *Strandkai | U 4 Überseequartier*

FROM ALTONA TO TEUFELS-BRÜCK

Hamburg is one of the greenest cities in Germany. And right here, in the west of the city, you can see why this is the case. There's one beautiful park after another, and between them mansions and villas and of course the world-famous avenue, the Elbchaussee.

But it isn't just the city's elite that has settled here. In places like Övelgönne many

It was once a railway station: Altona city hall

SIGHTSEEING FROM ALTONA TO TEUFELSBRÜCK

1 Altonaer Balkon

2 Altonaer Museum

ordinary families continue to live even today, the descendants of captains and pilots who built their pretty houses along the banks of the Elbe. And Ottensen too offers something different: narrow streets, workers' houses, pubs, numerous shops and a beautiful cinema will tempt you to go on an extended shopping spree until well into the evening. Call in and see the Altonaer Museum. And, should you happen to get up early on Sundays, the fish market is open from 5am in summer.

1 ALTONAER BALKON ☼
(135 E5) (𝟙 H7)

This is a great vantage point and a popular meeting place for boules players and barbecue enthusiasts. In the distance you can see the 500m/1640ft long Köhlbrandbrücke, a bridge which spans the Köhlbrand

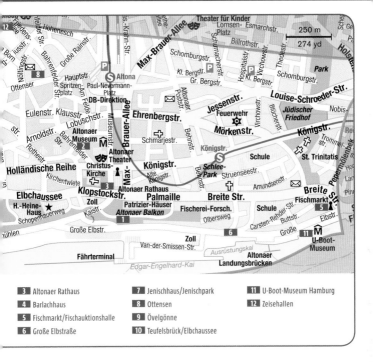

3 Altonaer Rathaus	**7** Jenischhaus/Jenischpark	**11** U-Boot-Museum Hamburg
4 Barlachhaus	**8** Ottensen	**12** Zeisehallen
5 Fischmarkt/Fischauktionshalle	**9** Övelgönne	
6 Große Elbstraße	**10** Teufelsbrück/Elbchaussee	

shipping lane 54m/177ft above the water; when completed in 1974, this cable-stayed bridge was a technical masterpiece; it is currently undergoing extensive renovation. The Altonaer Balkon is a good starting point for a walk. To the right, you can walk along the Elbe to Wedel in a couple of hours and, to the left, you can make your way into the city centre. Either way you'll be following the INSIDERTIP Elbhöhenweg, a 23km/14mi path (not always signposted). *Palmaille/Klopstockplatz | bus and S-Bahn Altona*

2 ALTONAER MUSEUM
(135 E5) (*∅ H7*)

A well-run institution. When it was about to be closed in 2010 due to lack of funds, a local action group occupied the rooms and organised sit-ins. There are barges,

old fish cutters and beautiful figureheads; model farmhouses and a fascinating permanent 'Elbe' exhibition with wonderfully old-fashioned dioramas. *Tue–Sun 10am–5pm | admission 6 euros | Museumstr. 23 | tel. 040 4 28 13 50 | www.altonaer museum.de | bus and S-Bahn Altona*

3 ALTONAER RATHAUS
(135 E5) (*∅ H7*)

'All to nah' to Hamburg (all too near), Altona was once a Danish district of the city. For centuries it provided a home to many religious refugees, today still seen in the names of the streets such as 'Große und Kleine Freiheit' (great and small liberty). In 1864, Altona became a part of Prussia. Between 1896 and 1898, the old railway station was converted into a magnificent, white town hall with an equestrian statue of Kaiser Wilhelm I in front. Today it is one of the city's most popular registry offices. By the way, Altona only became part of Hamburg in 1937 with the so-called 'Greater Hamburg Act'. *Bus and S-Bahn Altona*

4 INSIDER TIP ► BARLACHHAUS
(133 F4) (*E6*)

This may be one of the nicest little museums in Hamburg. Werner Kallmorgen's modest building in the centre of Jenisch park is noteworthy for its clean lines. It now houses the magnificent collection of the Hamburg patron (and former tobacco magnate) Hermann F. Reemtsma. The sculptor Ernst Barlach was ostracised and persecuted by the Nazis but Reemtsma was undeterred and continued to give him commissions. *Tue–Sun 11am–6pm | admission 6 euros | Baron-Voght-Str. 50 a | tel. 040 82 60 85 | www.ernst-barlach-haus. de | metro bus 15 Hochrad*

5 FISCHMARKT/FISCHAUKTIONS-HALLE ● (135 F5) (*J7*)

There are said to be Hamburgers who have never visited the fish market; for others it is a ritual end to their party or pub crawl. It's a very entertaining experience with lots of colourful characters; the banter employed by the fruit and fish sellers may not be the politest but they put on a great show, and even by 6am there's usually a huge throng of visitors. As well as fish and seafood there are stalls selling fruit and vegetables, and the pot plants for 5 euros make a nice souvenir *(Sun, April–Oct 5am–9.30am, Nov–March 7am–9.30am)*. The best place to enjoy a Sunday brunch is in the Fischauktionshalle (auction hall), which was constructed by the Altona merchants in 1895 as a 'cathedral to fish'. *Bus 111 Fischauktionshalle*

6 GROSSE ELBSTRASSE
(135 E–F 5–6) (*H–J7*)

It is a few years ago now that this street was notorious for kerb crawling. Today it's lined not by prostitutes and their clients but by one new building after another. The PR people call it a 'pearl necklace on the Elbe', though many of the 'pearls' remain empty. It's the same old story: glass, concrete and astronomical rents. Nevertheless a walk from the fish market to Övelgönne is still interesting and there are a number of nice restaurants. Designed by Hadi Teherani and completed in 2005, the ● 🌿 INSIDER TIP *Dockland* is a spectacular office building, whose shape resembles a ship. You can climb the 140 steps onto the 'bridge' – the roof – where you'll be rewarded with

Fish fresh off the boat at the Fischmarkt

sensational views. *S 1, 3 Königstraße | bus 111 Große Elbstraße*

▇7 JENISCHHAUS/JENISCHPARK ★
(133 F4–5) *(⌖ E6–7)*

Even at an early stage, the western part of Hamburg became the desired residential area for wealthy merchants. Jenisch House is one of the most beautiful, English-style, mansions from that time. Even Prussia's leading architect Karl Friedrich Schinkel was involved in the planning. The living rooms have been preserved in their original state and, today, form the core of the Museum of Art and Culture on the Elbe. *Tue–Sun 11am–6pm | admission 5 euros | admission with the neighbouring Barlachhaus 8 euros | Baron-Voght-Str. 50a | tel. 040 82 87 90 | metro bus 15 Hochrad.* The eponymous park was also laid out in the English style. In around 1800 Baron Caspar Voght had the land developed into an agricultural model estate and at the same time created the wonderful land-scaped park with views of the Elbe. There's a pleasant walk leading from the Teufels-brück quay to the new botanical garden at the Klein Flottbek S-Bahn station.

▇8 INSIDER⧉TIP OTTENSEN
(135 D–E 4–5) *(⌖ H6–7)*

This was always (and will hopefully long remain) Hamburg's liveliest district. The colourful mélange is unique in the city. Punks and pensioners, yuppies and eco-warriors – everyone lives here peacefully side by side. In Ottensen you can find some of the city's nicest restaurants, as well as unusual shops, delicatessens, cafés, fashion boutiques, pubs, Turkish snack stalls and trendy bars. For decades all attempts by estate agents and the property developers to harmonise the attractive hotch-potch by putting up boring new buildings have failed. *Bus and S-Bahn Altona*

Elegant interior: Jenischhaus

▇9 ÖVELGÖNNE ★
(134 B–C5) *(⌖ F–G7)*

In addition to Blankenese this is the most popular weekend destination for Hamburg's sun worshippers. The picturesque row of old captains' and ship pilots' houses on the banks of the Elbe is only a few hundred metres long. If you want to live here, you probably have to marry into one of the families; they guard their traditions tightly. That is why you should be discreet and not get caught pressing your nose too closely to the windowpanes. Don't miss a visit to the ● INSIDER⧉TIP *Strandperle (Övelgönne 60 | daily in summer, Sat/Sun in winter)*, a great beach bar right on the Elbe: feet in the sand, glass in your hand, watching the ships go by. You will find wonderful old ships in the *Museumshafen Övelgönne (free admission | www.museums hafen-oevelgoenne.de)*, and an old Hadag steamer has been converted into a café. If you see people milling around there don't be afraid to speak to them, they're only too pleased to meet outsiders. Under the glass dome on the roof of the Augustinum old age home is ☀ *Café Elbwarte (Tue, Thu and Sat/Sun 3–6pm)*. The view is well worth it. A walk from here to Teufelsbrück takes about 90 minutes. *Bus 112 Neumühlen*

🔟 TEUFELSBRÜCK/ELBCHAUSSEE
(133 F5) (*ØD7*)

At Flottbek an der Elbe a stream once flowed into the Elbe river. The old bridge that crossed it was called the Teufelsbrücke (devil's bridge) after the neighbouring wooded area known as the Duwels Bomgarde, which with its marshy lowlands was considered to be a sinister place. The Count of Schauenburg, who once ruled in these parts, sold the land to a citizen of Hamburg; today the Teufelsbrück quay lies about halfway along Hamburg's most famous street, the Elbchaussee. In the days gone by, one went by horse and carriage on an outing to the 'Café zum Bäcker'; today, a convertible is the preferred mode of transport and one drinks one's espresso on the terrace of the famous *Louis C. Jacob* hotel (→ p. 64, 94). The poet Detlev von Liliencron once called the Elbchaussee 'the most beautiful road in the world'. But for some time now the image of Hamburg's premier address has been severely dented. The traffic, especially on weekends with all the daytrippers, is terrible. In addition, uniform blocks of flats were thrown up in the old parks; some ugly, some pretentious, some both. And finally along came the Airbus, and from their expensive balconies residents now look straight across at the runway. How annoying! But the tourists were

BOOKS & FILMS

▶ **The Beatles in Hamburg: The Stories the Scene and How it All Began** – Spencer Leigh's sensitive account conveys not only the story of the Beatles in Hamburg but also the whole spirit of the age (2011)

▶ **The Wanted Man** – John le Carre switches to a post-Cold War scenario in this 2009 novel set entirely in Hamburg, involving the war on terror and plenty of spying and intrigue

▶ **Inferno: The Devastation of Hamburg, 1943** – Keith Lowe's account of the Hamburg air raids and the build up to them is as shocking as it is moving, as it reveals the full extent of the hellish reality unleashed on the city's population (2012)

▶ **Odessa File** – Frederick Forsyth's novel about a young journalist's attempt to track down a former SS concentration camp commander is partly set in Hamburg. Locations for the 1974 film include the Alter Elbtunnel, Große Freiheit and the Reeperbahn

▶ **Soul Kitchen** – Fatih Akin's 2009 comedy about a lovesick Greek cook from Wilhelmsburg. It is a real homage to Hamburg, the settings ranging from Le Canard Nouveau on the Elbchaussee to the Speicherstadt and out to the Astra Stube nightclub beneath the Sternbrücke

One of the nicest places along the Elbchaussee is the lime tree shaded Hotel Jacob terrace

happy: when the A 380 first came in to land on the opposite side of the Elbe the Hotel Jacob was booked out! *Express bus 36, 39 | metro bus 21 | bus 286 | Hadag ferry 64 Anleger Teufelsbrück*

🔢 U-BOOT-MUSEUM HAMBURG
(135 F6) *(Ø J7)*

It is a bit eerie, but very real: the 92m/300ft long U-434 Russian submarine was launched in Nizhny Novgorod in 1976 and was operational all over the world as a spy vessel. It now occupies a prominent berth right by the fish market. If you are not claustrophobic, take a look inside. *Daily from 10 or 11am until evening, according to season | admission 9 euros | St.-Pauli-Fischmarkt 10 | www.U-434.de | bus 111 Fischauktionshalle*

🔢 INSIDER TIP ZEISEHALLEN
(135 D4) *(Ø H6)*

Dating from 1865, the former Zeise factory buildings, which produced ships' propellers, were converted in 1988 into a modern cultural centre incorporating a cinema, galleries, and the university's Institute of Theatre, Musical Theatre and Film. At the time the project was seen as a real innovation and became a model for many similar schemes in Hamburg. If you're interested you could, for example, make for the Otto-von-Bahren Park, where the enormous site of an old gas works has just been wonderfully transformed into living spaces. *Friedensallee | metro bus 2 Friedensallee*

GRINDEL-VIERTEL/ EPPENDORF

The districts described here lie on the western shores of the Alster. Planten un Blomen, the large park that occupies the former ramparts, is Hamburg's green lung.

You can enjoy a beer with students at the university campus, learn about foreign cultures at the Museum of Ethnology, admire the Grindel tower blocks and their

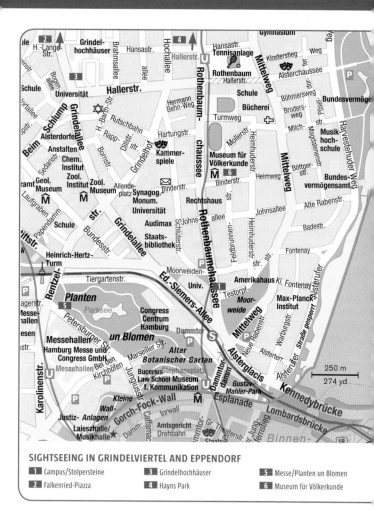

SIGHTSEEING IN GRINDELVIERTEL AND EPPENDORF

1 Campus/Stolpersteine

2 Falkenried-Piazza

3 Grindelhochhäuser

4 Hayns Park

5 Messe/Planten un Blomen

6 Museum für Völkerkunde

place in Hamburg's architectural history or have a glass of prosecco at one of the fashionable Italian bars in chic Eppendorf.

1 CAMPUS/STOLPERSTEINE
(136 C2) (∅ L5)

The university is located in the Grindel district, where 40,000 students liven up the pubs and squares. Here you can also find Germany's oldest repertoire cinema (*Abaton*) and many lovely old town houses. Before World War II, Hamburg was home to more than 30,000 Jews, and one-third of them lived here in the Grindel district. The main synagogue was located on Bornplatz. It and other synagogues in the district were destroyed by fire on the 'Night of Broken Glass' on 9 November 1938, from which time Jewish life in Grindel was systematically eradicated. Look out for the INSIDER TIP 'Stolpersteine' (stumbling blocks), small brass plaques set into the pavement in front of the houses in remembrance of those who were deported and murdered. Hamburg's most famous chief rabbi Joseph Carlebach lived at Hallerstraße 76 until his deportation. *Grindelhof/ Schlüterstraße | metro bus 4, 5 Grindelhof | U 1 Hallerstraße*

2 FALKENRIED-PIAZZA
(128 B6) (*Ⓜ L3*)

Piazza? That sounds chic – just as chic as the apartments that have been built on the site of an old tram depot. Old and new have been tastefully combined here, and there are pubs and shops too. With the award and certificate to prove it, the neighbourhood is officially among the nicest in Hamburg. The adjacent Isebek Canal is a great place to relax and unwind. Some old workers' houses still stand between Löwenstrasse and Falkenried. The alternative appeal of their shared gardens and tennants' action groups makes

them something quite special! *U 3 Hoheluftbrücke, Eppendorfer Baum*

3 GRINDELHOCHHÄUSER
(136 B–C1) (*Ⓜ L4*)

They were a real sensation: Hamburg's first postwar tower blocks. Each of the 12 blocks of flats is 200m/656ft long and they are described in the architectural lexicon as the 'reincarnation of the buried ideals of the 1920s'. In the nearby district office *(Grindelberg 66)* there is still an old INSIDER TIP paternoster lift in operation. *metro bus 5 Bezirksamt Eimsbüttel*

4 HAYNS PARK (128 C4) (*Ⓜ L2*)

This is a delightful corner of Eppendorf with the Alster flowing by. It is said that the theatre director and film star Gustav Gründgens used to rehearse his roles in the small round temple here. In summer people compete for the best barbecue and picnic spots along the Alster, children splash around in the paddling pools and they all shoo the geese that – to put it delicately – leave their droppings all over the place. This is also the location of

The 'stumbling blocks' in memory of deported Jewish residents of the Grindel district

Hamburg's oldest boathouse, which has been a meeting place for canoeists ever since 1874: the *Bootshaus Silwar (Eppendorfer Landstr. 148 b | tel. 040 47 62 07 | www.bootshaus-silwar.com)*. If you want to try something different you can always rent a pedalo in the shape of a swan *(boats from 10 euros per hour)*. Metro bus 20, 22, 25 Eppendorf Markt

5 MESSE/PLANTEN UN BLOMEN
(124 B–C1) (*M L5*)

Hamburg's green lung – 'plants and flowers' in English – lies right next to the trade fair grounds, which have just been extended as far as the TV tower. In the Middle Ages the ramparts were used to defend the city, but in the mid 19th century they were transformed into a green park. The greenhouses are a remnant of the days when this was Hamburg's only botanical garden. The new botanical garden is located in Flottbek, but with its plants, lakes and ponds, fountains, the Japanese garden, miniature golf and trampoline area, Planten un Blomen still has a lot to offer. It is wonderful to be able to relax on the wooden seats in the summer. There is a large ice skating rink behind the Hamburg Museum *(→ p. 36)* that is used by in-line skaters in summer; and there are playgrounds dotted around the park, the best one being on the corner of Marseiller Straße/St Petersburger Straße, which offers pony rides in the summer. *May–Sept daily 7am–11pm, Oct–April 7am–9pm | www.plantenunblomen.hamburg.de | U 1 Stephansplatz | U 2 Messehallen*

6 MUSEUM FÜR VÖLKERKUNDE
(136 C2) (*M L5*)

This is one of the largest ethnological collections in Germany, and even the building, constructed in 1907–10, is impressive. The imposing entrance hall is decorated with art nouveau features. The INSIDER TIP hall with masks from the South Seas is great – it's amazing to see what can be made out of grass and coconuts. And there's also a realistic-looking pharaoh's

Planten un Blomen: ideal for a break from the big city bustle

grave that you have to descend into. A family-friendly establishment. *Tue–Sun 10am–6pm, Thu 10am–9pm | admission 7 euros | tel. 040 4 28 87 90 | www.voelker kundemuseum.com | Rothenbaumchaussee 64 | U 1 Hallerstraße*

MORE SIGHTS

BALLINSTADT (141 F4) (*Ø O*)

A total of about 5 million people have left Hamburg for other parts of the world. Many of them spent their last weeks on German soil in the barracks of the so-called Auswandererstadt (emigration city) on the Veddel, which the former Hapag boss Albert Ballin had built at the end of the 19th century. Nothing here is that old, but the three halls have been reconstructed using the original plans. It's a very interesting museum with many details on the often tragic history of emigration. You can look for your forebears on a computer: all the passenger lists since 1840 are available. A pleasant – and appropriate – way to get there is with the INSIDER TIP Maritime Circle Line, whose launches call in at many stops around the harbour. Departure from the shipping piers *(pier 10 | day ticket 9.50 euros | tel. 040 28 49 39 63 | www.maritime-circle-line.de). Museum: daily 10am–6pm, Nov–March until 4.30pm (last admission one hour before closing) | admission 12 euros | Veddeler Bogen 2 | www.ballinstadt.de | S 3, 31 Veddel-Ballinstadt*

INSIDER TIP HAFENMUSEUM
(141 D3) (*Ø M8*)

The harbour museum includes a floating steam crane, a dredger and an assortment of old working vessels. In the shed there's an exhibition about dock working. From the end of the quay you look across to HafenCity. *Easter–Oct Thu–Sun 10am–*

6pm | admission 5 euros | Australiastraße | www.museum-der-arbeit.de | S-Bahn 3, 31 Veddel-Ballinstadt, then bus 256 Hafenmuseum

IMTECH-ARENA/HSV-MUSEUM
(126 B–C5) (*Ø F3*)

You can get a good idea of the ups and downs of real fans of Hamburg's famous football team in the HSV Museum, and you can also book a tour of the stadium. *Daily 10am–5.30pm | admission 6, with tour 8 euros | tour daily at varying times | Sylvesterallee 7 | tel. 040 41 55 15 50 | www.hsv-museum.de | shuttle bus from Stellingen S-Bahn station only during events*

JARRESTADT (129 F5) (*Ø N3*)

In 1909, Fritz Schumacher became the city of Hamburg's building director. In the ensuing years up to his retirement in 1933 he changed the face of the city like nobody else before or since. As well as an architect he was a far-sighted urban designer who planned for the needs of millions of people, including the model estate of Jarrestadt which was built in 1927–30. Partially destroyed during the war it was reconstructed and remains a popular place to live to this day. If you'd like to know more take a tour with the INSIDER TIP A-Tour's architecture experts *(group advance bookings: tel. 040 23 93 97 17 | a-tour.de/en/home/home.html). Between Jarrestraße, Wiesendamm and Goldbekufer | bus 172 Jarrestraße*

MUSEUM DER ARBEIT
(130 B5) (*Ø P3*)

Participation is what this labour museum is all about: on the premises of the former New York Hamburg Rubber Goods Company you (and your children) can get actively involved – in a printing shop, for example *(Mon 6pm–9pm)*. You can reach the museum by boat from Jungfernstieg

(April–Oct Sat/Sun 4 departures | single journey 6.5 euros). Mon 1pm–9pm, Tue–Sat 10am–5pm, Sun 10am–6pm | admission 6 euros | Wiesendamm 3 | tel. 040 4 28 13 33 40 | www.museum-der-arbeit. de | S-/U-Bahn Barmbek

'Fate' by Hugo Lederer at the Ohlsdorf cemetery

OHLSDORFER FRIEDHOF ★
(130–131 B–D1) *(𝄐 O)*

The largest landscaped cemetery in the world is much more than just a final resting place for the dead – it is an excursion destination in its own right. The benches under the large old trees are perfect for pondering over our worldly existence. The *crematorium (Talstraße | near the main entrance)* built by Fritz Schumacher between 1930–1932 is architecturally outstanding. One year later, Hamburg's building director was ousted by the Nazis. Many prominent Germans lie buried here and with 200,000 graves and an area of over 900 acres, there is plenty to see. There is an information centre, a small museum and you can also download tips for tours from the internet. *April–Oct daily 8am–9pm, Nov–March 8am–6pm | main entrance Fuhlsbütteler Str. 756 | www.friedhof-hamburg.de/start-english/ohlsdorf-cemetery | S-/U-Bahn Ohlsdorf*

INSIDER TIP ▶ SAMMLUNG FALCKENBERG
(142 C4) *(𝄐 O)*

This inspired collection of modern art is housed in an old tyre factory in Harburg. Something like this is normally only found in New York and naturally Berlin. A few of the rooms are taken up by the bizarre works of Jonathan Meese, and the private collection of the patron Harald Falckenberg is now a satellite of the Deichtorhallen. *Guided tour only with prior booking, done via the website | admission/tour 15 euros | tel. 040 32 50 67 62 | www.sammlung-falckenberg.de/?site_language=EN | S 1, 31 Harburg Rathaus, then on foot*

STADTPARK/PLANETARIUM
(129 E4) *(𝄐 N2)*

Fritz Schumacher also put his stamp on the Stadtpark (city park); the site was planned with military precision. The former hunting grounds of the landowner Adolf Sierich were to be transformed into an open-air 'house of the people' and that is what it remains to this day: on Sundays people gather on the large lawn to play sports, there's a beer garden, a natural swimming pool, an enormous playground and the *Planetarium*. You can learn everything you need to know in order to explain the stars to your children, and much else besides, for after all this is one of the most modern planetariums in Europe. Call in advance as it's often sold out! *Entrance and observation deck Tue–Sun from 9am, several shows daily | tickets from 9.50 euros | Hindenburgstr. 1 b | tel. 040 42 88 65 20 | www.planetarium-hamburg.de/service/information-for-our-english-speaking-visitors | U 3 Borgweg, then 10 min on foot*

TRIPS & TOURS

ALTES LAND (142 A–B3) (*Ø O*)

When the apples blossom in the spring it's really gorgeous here. Altes Land is the largest single fruit-growing area in Northern Europe. In this case 'Alt' has nothing to do with the German word for 'old'. The first settlers here came from the Netherlands and 'Olland' was the original Low German name for this region. This gradually developed from 'olles Land' into 'Altes Land'. The small villages have charming names like Francop, Jork, Ladekop and Cranz and, with their houses built on dykes, they really are reminiscent of Dutch coastal villages. You can take lovely strolls along the dykes and look across the Elbe to Blankenese or Wedel; they are also ideal for skating or cycling along. A nice place to take a break is the *Obsthof Matthies (daily | Am Elbdeich 31 | tel. 04162 9 15 80 | www.obsthof.de)* just beyond Jork. And a great place to watch the boats and eat sausage is the *Lühe (Grünen Deich)* jetty, where cyclists congregate in the summer. For further information about the Altes Land: *www.tourismus-altesland.de*. *By car or bike and ferry 64 from the Landungsbrücken to Finkenwerder, then a cycle tour as far as Steinkirchen*

HARBURGER BERGE

(142 C4) (*Ø O*)

It might be difficult to believe but there are also mountains around Hamburg and the restaurants are indeed called 'Berghütten' (mountain huts). Hamburgers come here to toboggan and even ski if there's enough snow. The *Fischbeker Heide (S 3, 31 Neugraben, then bus 250 Fischbeker Heideweg)*, little sister of the Lüneburger Heide (Lüneburg Heath) is a wonderful area, with its moorland and hiking trails. If the children start whining, you can always continue to the *Wildpark Schwarze Berge (daily 8am–6pm, in winter 9am–5pm | admission 9 euros | Am Wildpark 1 | Rosengarten | www.wildpark-schwarze-berge.de)* home to wolves, lynx and bats and, most importantly, the comic potbellied pigs that grunt along behind you if you have brought the right food. Right next door is the open-air museum *Freilichtmuseum Am Kiekeberg (Tue–Fri 10am–6pm | 9 euros | Am Kiekeberg 1 | Rosengarten-Ehestorf | www.kiekeberg-museum.de | S 3, 31 Neuwiedenthal, then bus 340 Wildpark or Museum Kiekeberg)*. Here they do everything from threshing to baking bread – there's always something going on.

SACHSENWALD (143 E–F3) (*Ø O*)

It was at *Schloss Friedrichsruh* castle in the Sachsenwald to the east of the city that the 'Iron Chancellor' Otto von Bismarck spent his twilight years. His descendants still live in the castle today and, just like their illustrious ancestor, they are closely watched by the press. You can take some great walks here, visit two museums and the *Butterfly Garden (20 March–Oct 10am–6pm | admission 7 euros | www.garten-der-schmetterlinge.de)* and finish off by enjoying a medallion of venison in the restaurant. *Bismarck Museum (Tue–Sun 10am–6pm, Nov–March until 4pm | admission 4 euros); Bismarck Foundation (Tue–Sun 10am–6pm, Nov–Feb until 5pm | in the old station | www.bismarckstiftung.de); Forsthaus Friedrichsruh restaurant (closed Mon | tel. 04104 69 23 66 | Budget). S 21 Aumühle*

FOOD & DRINK

The regional cuisine includes fish from the Elbe and the North Sea, fruit from orchards of the Altes Land region and cabbage from Dithmarschen.

Fortunately people in Hamburg like to eat well. Whether it's champagne soup, calamaretti or Barbary duck: the menus in the better restaurants in Hamburg leave nothing to be desired. As a result, Hamburg has (quite rightly) the reputation of being the best (even if not the cheapest) city in Germany for eating out. A willingness to try out new dishes and the influx of people from different corners of the world have both had an impact on Hanseatic tastes. Whether it's Italian, Viennese or Portu-

guese, everyone likes to try out new places here. And what really counts – surprise, surprise – is a view of the Elbe or Alster. For the privilege of dining along the river between the fish market and Övelgönne, for example, you will usually have to dig deeper into your pocket. The small bistros and snack bars where the chef in person does the cooking are usually very good. There is an abundance of such eateries in Ottensen, in the side streets of St Pauli or in the Karo district. For a long time now many chefs have used only regional and organic produce, and there are more and more vegetarian dishes to be found on the menus. At the top end of the scale you

Photo: Restaurant Rive

Plaice on the banks of the Elbe or a neighbourhood *currywurst*? Above all it's the view that's important in Hamburg!

should definitely reserve a table well in advance – at least when it's the weekend. One tip for all those who enjoy good food: almost all top restaurants have excellent and moderately priced lunch menus. However, they are then usually closed for the afternoon. Cheaper restaurants provide hot meals throughout the day. Most cafés open at between 9am and 11am; the same goes for snack bars and bistros.

CAFÉS & ICE CREAM PARLOURS

ALEX IM ALSTERPAVILLON ☆ (125 D3) (*Ɱ L6*)

The pavilion dates from 1953 and is the seventh to be built on this site. During the Nazi period it was a meeting place for Hamburg's young jazz scene – it was their way of rebelling against the regime. The

An institution in the Eppendorf district: Café Lindtner

guests today make quite a noise too, but without the jazz. *Daily | Jungfernstieg 54 | tel. 040 3 50 18 70 | S-/U-Bahn Jungfernstieg*

INSIDER TIP BODO'S BOOTSSTEG
(137 D2) (*ω M5*)

The nicest spot on the Alster: many people come to enjoy their lunch break in the old deckchairs. Bodo Windeknecht looks after the boat hire while his son manages the café. *Daily, in winter weekends only | Bootssteg Rabenstraße | tel. 040 4 10 35 25 | bus 109 Böttgerstraße*

CAFÉ KOPPEL ☺ (137 E4) (*ω N6*)

Late risers are in their element here, because they serve breakfast until 10pm. Everything is vegetarian, lots of it organic and the prices are fair. They open up the garden in summer. After a bite to eat you can take a stroll through the art and craft galleries of *Koppel 66*. *Daily | Lange Reihe 75 | tel. 40 24 92 35 | metro bus 6 Gurlittstraße*

CAFÉ LEONAR ★ (136 C2) (*ω L4*)

One of the most interesting cafés in the city in the old Jewish quarter of Grindel. Kosher food, a cultural programme with Jewish emphasis, lots of magazines to read: the perfect place to think about life and everything else. Breakfast served daily until 3pm, all day Sun. *Daily | Grindelhof 59 (until spring 2014 Grindelhof 87) | tel. 040 41 35 30 11 | www.cafeleonar.de | metro bus 4, 5 Grindelhof*

CAFÉ LINDTNER (128 C5) (*ω L3*)

A wooden revolving door leads into the panelled elegance of this traditional German coffee shop; even ladies from posh Othmarschen come here for the Maharani gateau (with cognac) and the delicious homemade chocolates. Breakfast buffet at the weekend. *Daily | Eppendorfer Landstr. 88 | tel. 040 4 80 60 00 | U 1,3 Kellinghusenstraße*

INSIDER TIP CAFÉ MIMOSA
(136 A4) (*ω K6*)

Espresso, fresh brioche, friendly service and the day's newspapers: this little café near the Reeperbahn is a favourite spot for the residents of St Pauli. *Closed Mon | Clemens-Schultz-Str. 87 | tel. 040 32 03 79 89 | U 3 St Pauli*

INSIDER TIP HERR MAX
(136 A3) (*ω K5*)

The 'in' cake shop in the Schanzen district: the petits fours are decorated with skulls, some of the cakes with skeletons! Don't be put off – the delicious cakes and chocolates are freshly made on site in keeping with the best confectioners' tradition. Packed out at weekends. *Daily | Schulterblatt 12 | tel. 040 69 21 99 51 | U 3 Feldstraße*

LAIB & LIEBE (135 E4–5) (*ഈ H6*)

This friendly café is situated to the east of Altona station on Große Bergstraße, which in the 1960s was celebrated as Germany's first shopping precinct. The first city branch of Ikea is due to open here in 2014. Observe the developments over a homemade lemonade or lunch. *Closed Sun | Große Bergstr. 243 | tel. 040 38 90 49 50 | bus and S-Bahn Altona*

LIEBLINGS EIS & CAFFÉ
(125 E4) (*ഈ M7*)

Ice cream parlour in the Chilehaus. Whether it's a sumptuously decorated ice cream creation you're after, a piece of cake or INSIDER TIP lemonade with fresh mint – everything here is homemade. *Closed Sun, in winter only Mon–Fri noon–5pm | Altstädterstraße 15 | tel. 040 79 41 67 96 | U 1 Meßberg*

MESSMER MOMENTUM
(124 C6) (*ഈ L7*)

Teatime in HafenCity: in the lounge of Germany's largest tea importer you can enjoy a pot of Earl Grey with scones while looking out over the Sandtorhafen. The *tea museum (free admission)* provides a lot of interesting facts about the noble beverage. The shop stocks more than 150 blends. *Daily | Am Kaiserkai 10 | tel. 040 73 67 90 00 | bus 111 Magellan-Terrassen*

TRANSMONTANA (136 A3) (*ഈ K5*)

Popular? This rather shabby looking place? Dead right! The Transmontana on the Schanze is the grandmother of all Portuguese *galão natas* joints (that's milk coffee and custard tarts, plus other Portuguese specialities). No matter how worn out the chairs or how long the queue: this is where real insiders enjoy their *galão*. *Daily | Schulterblatt 86 | metro bus 15 Schulterblatt*

WITTHÜS TEESTUBEN (132 C4) (*ഈ C6*)

For afternoon tea in Blankenese try the idyllic surroundings of this thatched villa

---

⭐ **Café Leonar**
Read the newspaper, chat, and ponder: this kosher café is popular amongst the intellectuals of the Grindel district → p. 62

⭐ **Fischereihafen-Restaurant**
A classic among seafood restaurants – in a lovely location on the Elbe → p. 66

⭐ **Bullerei**
German TV chef Tim Mälzer in his element → p. 67

⭐ **Nil**
Trendy place with great food; youthful and lively → p. 69

⭐ **Schauermann**
Count the container ships going past from the retro 60s style chairs → p. 69

⭐ **Le Canard Nouveau**
Ali Güngörmüs' delectable cuisine on the Elbe → p. 64

⭐ **Louis C. Jacob**
One of the best chefs in the city and a personable host → p. 64

⭐ **Seven Seas Süllberg**
Beer garden and Michelin star restaurant with superb views from the banks of the Elbe at Blankenese → p. 64

MARCO POLO HIGHLIGHTS

in the middle of a deer park. With your tea you can have, for example, cherry rum cake with fruit and cream. The gourmet restaurant starts serving at 7pm. *Tearoom Tue–Sun 2pm–6pm, Sun brunch from 10am (reservations only) | Elbchaussee 499a | tel. 040 86 01 73 | S 1 Blankenese | metro bus 1 and 22 Mühlenberg*

SNACK BARS

BRÜCKE 10 ● (136 A5–6) (*∅ K7*)
This is the place to come for fabulous (and generous) shrimp rolls. Great atmosphere and friendly staff. *Daily | at the St Pauli Landungsbrücken/pier 10 | St Pauli | tel. 040 65 04 68 99 | S-/U-Bahn Landungsbrücken*

CURRY QUEEN (128 C4) (*∅ L2*)
According to the influential French Gault Millau restaurant guide, this chic snack bar in Eppendorf serves up the best *currywurst* in Germany. The 🕒 veal sausage is organic and there are hints of hibiscus or lemon grass. You don't get chips, but potato salads and desserts instead. *Closed Sun/Mon | Erikastr. 50 | tel. 040 52 67 77 84 | metro bus 20, 22, 25 Eppendorfer Marktplatz*

GOURMET RESTAURANTS

Le Canard Nouveau ⭐ 🍃
(134 C5) (*∅ G7*)
Ali Güngörmüs cooks exquisite gourmet cuisine yet keeps his feet on the ground despite all the famous names he meets and greets. His lovely restaurant on Elbchaussee was designed by Hamburg's star architect Meinhard von Gerkan, whose offices occupy the top floors. Set menus from 79 euros. *Closed Mon, Sat/Sun evenings only | Elbchaussee 139 | tel. 040 88 12 95 31 | www.lecanard-hamburg.de | metro bus 15 | express bus 36 Hohenzollernring*

Haerlin (125 D3) (*∅ L6*)
This is how the true Hanseatic family loves to dine: in nice tasteful surroundings but with top-notch food. The restaurant has two Michelin stars and the service is perfect. Set menus from 105 euros. *Evenings only, closed Sun/Mon | Neuer Jungfernstieg 9 | tel. 040 34 94 33 10 | www.hvj.de | S-/U-Bahn Jungfernstieg*

Louis C. Jacob ⭐ 🍃 **(133 E5)** (*∅ D6*)
With two Michelin stars Thomas Martin is the best chef in town. The hotel restaurant has a dignified Hanseatic ambience, and a lovely terrace with view of the Elbe in the summer. But leave room for petits fours with your after dinner coffee! Set menus from 89 euros. *Closed Mon/Tue | Elbchaussee 401 | tel. 040 82 25 55 23 | www.hotel-jacob.de | express bus 36 | bus 286 Sieberlingstraße*

Seven Seas Süllberg ⭐ 🍃
(132 A5) (*∅ B6*)
On the Süllberg in Blankenese it is not only the view that is exceptional but also what Karlheinz Hauser produces in the kitchen (recently been awarded with two Michelin stars). Have a look in the ballroom and in the summer visit the beer garden high above the Elbe. Set menus from 79 euros. *Closed Mon/Tue (restaurant deck daily) | Süllbergterrasse 12 | tel. 040 8 66 25 20 | www.suellberg-hamburg.de | express bus 48 Kahlkamp*

Hanseatic style, culinary perfection: Louis C. Jacob on the Elbchaussee

INSIDER TIP ESSZIMMER
(136 A2) *(□ J4)*
Sooo tasty and sooo popular! One of the best lunches in town, and half of Eimsbüttel and the rest of Hamburg seem to know it. *Closed Sun | Eppendorfer Weg 73 | tel. 040 89 00 69 00 | metro bus 20, 25 Fruchtallee*

JIM BLOCK (125 D4) *(□ L6)*
Without its Block restaurants many a Hamburg family would go hungry: steak and chips for the lads, baked potatoes and sour cream for the lasses. Always full. *Daily | Jungfernstieg 1 | tel. 040 30 38 22 17 | S-/U-Bahn Jungfernstieg*

TEUFELS KÜCHE
(135 D4) *(□ H6)*
From the very outset an 'in' place to go, this is almost a 'gourmet' snack bar. Specialities include homemade lamb sausages and pasta. *Daily | Ottenser Hauptstr. 47 | tel. 040 39 80 49 77 | bus and S-Bahn Altona*

VERRÜCKT NACH FRISCH
(128 B6) *(□ K3)*
Thorsten and Sina are themselves vegetarians and love everything that is fresh – and that's exactly what they serve in their pleasant café-restaurant: soups, salads, quiches and cakes. In summer they put tables out on Falkenried Piazza. *Mon–Fri 8.30am–6pm, Sat 9.30am–6pm | Straßenbahnring 19 | tel. 040 42 93 60 00 | U 3 Hoheluftbrücke*

RESTAURANTS: EXPENSIVE

BROOK (125 D5) *(□ M7)*
Minimalist ambience as a contrast to the great view of the Speicherstadt. Chef Lars Schablinski serves haute cuisine and im-

Steffen Henssler in his element – rolling sushi in Henssler Henssler

aginative fish dishes. *Closed Sun | Bei den Mühren 91 | tel. 040 37 50 31 28 | www. brook-restaurant.de | U 1 Meßberg*

CARLS (124 C6) (*ℳ L7*)

Located in HafenCity, Carls is an offshoot of the Louis C. Jacob Hotel on the Elbchaussee. Light snacks are available in the bistro at the front, complete with views of the Elbphilharmonie building site; in the chic restaurant at the back you can enjoy expensive dishes with views over the Elbe. *Daily | Am Kaiserkai 69 | tel. 040 3 00 32 24 00 | www.carls-brasserie.de | bus 111 Am Kaiserkai*

FISCHEREIHAFEN-RESTAURANT ★ ☆ (135 E6) (*ℳ H7*)

Celebrities eat so regularly with the Kowalke family that chef Rüdiger is now part of the VIP crowd himself. But what is more important is that his fish dishes are exquisite. Ask for a table by the window! *Daily | Große Elbstr. 143 | tel. 040 38 18 16 | www.fischereihafenrestaurant. de | bus 111 Fährterminal Altona*

HENSSLER HENSSLER (135 E6) (*ℳ J7*)

Steffen Henssler is also a German TV chef and likes to be the centre of attention. But his food is what counts: try the sushi rolls or tuna steak. The acoustics in the old warehouse, however, take some getting used to. *Closed Sun | Große Elbstr. 160 | tel. 040 38 69 90 00 | www.henssler henssler.de/#/startseite | bus 111 Sandberg*

MESS (124 A2) (*ℳ K6*)

This little cellar restaurant in the Karo district is proof positive that Mediterranean cuisine can indeed combine with dishes such as *Wiener schnitzel*. **INSIDER TIP** Inexpensive lunch menu. *Closed Sun, Sat evenings only | Turnerstr. 9 | tel. 040 43 41 23 | www.mess.de | U 3 Feldstraße*

RIVE ☆ (135 E6) (*ℳ J7*)

Rive was the first restaurant on this stretch of the Elbe to become popular with the trendy crowd. The most important question then and now: where do all the gorgeous waiters and waitresses come from? When it's full it does get a bit hectic. *Daily |*

Van-der-Smissen-Str. 1 | tel. 040 3 80 59 19 | www.rive.de | bus 111 Große Elbstraße

VLET ✹ (125 D6) (*m M7*)

For some restaurant critics this is a real hotspot in the Speicherstadt/HafenCity area, for others it's just another example of how everything here is more chic and expensive. However, the fact remains that the food is good and the atmosphere in the old warehouse great. *Closed Sun, Sat evening only | Am Sandtorkai 23, via the exterior spiral staircase | tel. 040 3 34 75 37 50 | www.vlet.de | bus 111 | metro bus 6 Am Sandtorquai*

RESTAURANTS: MODERATE

ATLAS (135 D3) (*m H5*)

Old factory buildings seem to attract good restaurants. That includes the Atlas in the Phoenixhof, a former industrial and commercial district in Ottensen. The great food is complimented by the friendly staff. *Sat evenings only, Sun brunch only 10.30am–3pm | Schützenstr. 9 a | in Phoenixhof | tel. 040 8 51 78 10 | metro bus 2 | bus 288 Schützenstraße (south)*

BISTRO VIENNA (136 A2) (*m K5*)

Can't be indiscreet here – the restaurant is tiny and everyone can hear every word – but that doesn't deter the regulars who come here to indulge in cod or boar ragout. No reservations so there may be a queue. *Evenings only from 7pm, closed Mon | Fettstr. 2 | tel. 040 4 39 91 82 | U 2 Christuskirche*

BOBBY REICH ✹ (129 D6) (*m M3*)

For generations those out for a stroll or 'to see and be seen' have been dropping in to eat here. The magnificent view over the Alster is uplifting, even if the drinks and homemade food are overpriced. *Daily | Fernsicht 2 | tel. 040 48 78 24 | bus 109 Harvestehuder Weg*

BRASSERIE LA PROVENCE (135 D5) (*m H6*)

Vive la France! Bright red walls, lavish décor and sumptuous food – tasty and cheerful. If you book you get an aperitif on the house. *Evenings only, closed Sun/ Mon | Eulenstr. 42 | tel. 040 30 60 34 07 | www.brasserielaprovence.de | metro bus 1 Große Brunnenstraße*

BULLEREI ★ (136 A3) (*m K5*)

Chef Tim Mälzer's most recent establishment, in the brick halls of the old abattoir in Schanzen, is just to the taste of his trendy clientele. Tip: despite the crush you'll always find a seat in the cheaper deli section at the front. The food is wholesome and very tasty *Daily | Lagerstr. 34 B | tel. 040 33 44 21 10 | www.bullerei.com | S-/U-Bahn Sternschanze*

CAFÉ PARIS (125 D4) (*m M7*)

For all lovers of French cuisine this is heaven! Of course all the waiters speak French, and the *steak frites* here really is *magnifique! Daily | Rathausstr. 4 | tel. 040 32 52 77 77 | U 3 Rathausmarkt*

COPPER HOUSE (136 A5) (*m K7*)

This large (it can seat 350 guests) Chinese restaurant has an open kitchen where you can see what's going on plus a self-service buffet. Difficult to imagine, but this huge place, which is always jam packed, is still a down-to-earth family-run business. *Daily | Davidstr. 37 | tel. 040 75 66 20 11 | S 1, 3 Reeperbahn*

CUNEO (136 A5) (*m K7*)

Italian dishes have been served up here since 1905, just like at mamma's. That seems to appeal just as much to the media crowd as to celebrities and tourists alike. *Evenings only, closed Sun | Davidstr. 11 | tel. 040 3125 80 | S 1, 3 Reeperbahn*

LOCAL SPECIALITIES

▶ **Aalsuppe** – the *aal* here is Low German 'everything' rather than *Aal* meaning 'eel'; so this is a typical soup made from leftovers, combining the sweet (prunes) with the savoury (bacon). If it does have real eel in it, then this is usually a concession to tourists.

▶ **Alsterwasser** – in other parts of Germany it's called *Radler*, in English shandy and that's exactly what it is: beer mixed with lemonade.

▶ **Birnen, Bohnen und Speck** – pears, green beans and bacon, together with potatoes, a kind of stew served in late summer.

▶ **Franzbrötchen** – tasty pastries with cinnamon, the perfect treat for a child that needs cheering up (photo right).

▶ **Hamburger Stubenküken** – they melt in the mouth, these spring chickens that weigh just 300–400g. They are usually roasted in the oven and served with morel mushrooms. They are called 'parlour chicks' as farmers used to keep them inside the house to protect them from the cold.

▶ **Labskaus** – salted meat, beetroot, pickled herring, onions and potatoes passed through the mincing machine and with a fried egg on top. Come on, be brave! It tastes better than it looks (photo left)!

▶ **Scholle Finkenwerder Art** – generally speaking, these are large fillets of plaice, coated with breadcrumbs and served with fried bacon and sautéed potatoes. Still a Sunday favourite among locals.

▶ **Stinte** – a tiny species of salmon that, for a few years now, is found locally again in the Elbe and has become a yuppie speciality. Fried in flour, you eat it whole, head, tail and all. Only available a few weeks in spring.

RESTAURANT ENGEL ✵
(133 F5) (*⑳ D7*)
Fantastic view of the ships sailing by from the Teufelsbrück quay. INSIDER TIP Brunch Sun. *Daily | tel. 040 82 41 87 | Anleger Teufelsbrück, Elbchaussee | express bus 36 | ferry 64 Teufelsbrück*

EISENSTEIN (135 D4) (*⑳ H6*)
First opened in the 1980s when Ottensen was still down-at-heel. Now the chic restaurant is a firmly established feature of the Zeisehallen. Delicious wood oven pizzas. *Daily | Friedensallee 9 | tel. 040 3 90 46 06 | metro bus 2 Friedensallee*

JUWELIER (136 A2) *(🗺 K5)*
Success story à la carte: young chef rents tiny premises, serves imaginative dishes such as guinea fowl with turnip and relies on local ingredients. Expect a queue. *Daily, evenings only | Weidenallee 27 | tel. 040 25 48 16 78 | S-/U-Bahn Sternschanze*

MARINEHOF (124 C4) *(🗺 L7)*
Nice, well-established restaurant with relaxed atmosphere and mixed clientele on the Fleetinsel, the island between the canals, shady outdoor terrace in the summer. *Closed Sun | Admiralitätstr. 77 | tel. 040 3 74 25 79 | S 1, 3 Stadthausbrücke*

LA MIRABELLE (136 B3) *(🗺 L5)*
The French chef is always in a good mood and the cheese trolley promises heavenly delights. Excellent little restaurant in the Grindel district. *Evenings only, closed Sun | Bundesstr. 15 | tel. 040 4 10 75 85 | metro bus 4, 5 Staatsbibliothek*

NIL ★ (136 A4) *(🗺 K6)*
Great organic cuisine in the hip atmosphere of an old shoe shop. And the kitchen staff never fails to come up with new ideas. *Evenings only, closed Tue | Neuer Pferdemarkt 5 | tel. 040 4 39 78 23 | U 3 Feldstraße*

OLD COMMERCIAL ROOM (124 B5) *(🗺 L7)*
The 'Michel' is across the way and the menu is in several languages for the many tourists who find their way to this venerable establishment. *Daily | Englische Planke 10 | tel. 040 36 63 19 | U 3 Baumwall*

LE PLAT DU JOUR (125 D4) *(🗺 M7)*
Jacques Lemercier, who once founded Hamburg's first gourmet restaurant, also has a more basic bistro: red tablecloths, good wines and very sensible prices, which explains why it's often full. *Daily | Dornbusch 4 | tel. 040 32 14 14 | U 3 Rathaus*

SCHAUERMANN ★ (136 A5) *(🗺 K7)*
Regulars of the anarchist pub *Onkel Otto*, the sports car clientele of the *Riverkasematten* and guests at the *Schauermann* all manage to coexist on this stretch of the Elbe where the fish market is. That the mixed neighbourhood functions at all is typical of Hamburg. The restaurant serves modern, light cuisine. *Evenings only, closed Sun | St.-Pauli-Hafenstr. 136 | tel. 040 31 79 46 60 | bus 112 St Pauli/Hafenstraße*

For food in the factory: the Eisenstein in Ottensen

SCHLACHTERBÖRSE (136 B3) *(🗺 K5)*
The central meat market is next door, and so you tend to get big helpings on your plate; photos of celebrity guests hang on the walls. *From 4pm, closed Sun | Kampstr. 42 | tel. 040 43 65 43 | U 3 Feldstraße*

WASSERSCHLOSS (125 E5) *(🗺 M7)*
The building on the tip of a promontory between two canals of the Speicherstadt

might resemble a small castle, but it was in fact home and workplace of the people who serviced and repaired the warehouse winches. Now it houses an extraordinary restaurant and absolutely amazing tea-shop. Just one of their specialities is tea-smoked fish. Nice Sunday brunch (booking essential). *Daily | Dienerreihe 4 | tel. 040 5 58 98 26 40 | U 1 Messberg*

RESTAURANTS: BUDGET

BARCELONA TAPAS (135 E5) *(𝄞 H7)*
Delicious: devils on horseback and roasted pepperoni. The simple, high-ceilinged rooms have a real Spanish atmosphere with all the tapas variations. Good choice of wine. *Evenings only, closed Sun | Max-Brauer-Allee 12 | tel. 040 38 08 36 35 | metro bus 15 | bus 112 Altonaer Rathaus*

DANIEL WISCHER (125 E4) *(𝄞 M6)*
Hamburg lads and lassies grew up with Daniel Wischer. Parents know there won't be any arguments because everyone likes the battered fish with delicious potato salad. Also a takeaway. *Mon–Sat 11am–8pm | Spitalerstr. 12 | tel. 040 32 52 58 15 | U 3 Mönckebergstraße*

ERIKAS ECK (136 B3) *(𝄞 K5)*
The opening times (kitchen open from 5pm–2pm!) might be a reason why night owls, early birds and taxi drivers find their way here for their meat loaf or steak. The corner restaurant is popular because of the generous portions of good simple fare. *Sat/Sun only until 9am | Sternstr. 98 | tel. 040 43 35 45 | U 3 Feldstraße*

INSIDER TIP ▶ OBERHAFEN-KANTINE (125 F6) *(𝄞 M7)*
The tiny brick building under the bridge leans alarmingly to one side. But it's nothing to worry about, the building dating from 1925 is solid enough; the former traditional snack bar has long been a listed building and today lures customers with its delicious Hamburg white sausages with herring or 'veiled peasant girl': toasted pumpernickel, chocolate and apple sauce. *Daily | Stockmeyerstr. 39 | tel. 040 32 80 99 84 | www.oberhafenkantine-hamburg.de | U 1 Meßberg*

PONTON OP'N BULLN ⚒
(132 B4) *(𝄞 B7)*
'Bulln' is what the residents of Blankenese call their quay. The nice snack bar there serves salmon cakes, soups and other goodies and is cheaper than the restau-

LOW BUDGET

▶ A reasonably priced lunch and lively theatre atmosphere is provided by *Die Kantine* **(125 F3)** *(𝄞 M6)* (*Mon–Fri 11.15am–3pm | Kirchenallee 39 | tel. 040 24 87 12 73 | S-/U-Bahn Hauptbahnhof*) in the Schauspielhaus. Guests eat in the front room while the rear is reserved for the ensemble.

▶ Some people would walk for miles for a pizza at *Slim Jim's* **(136 A4)** *(𝄞 K6)* (*daily, Sat/Sun only from 1pm | Bei der Schilleroper 1–3 | U 3 Feldstraße*): ultra-thin crust, standard price 5.50 euros plus favourite topping.

▶ Between noon and 3pm the young chefs at *Slowman* **(125 E5)** *(𝄞 M7)* (*Burchardstr. 13 C | in the Chilehaus | tel. 040 33 75 61 | U 1 Steinstraße*) prepare reasonably priced lunches. TV and Michelin-starred chef Christian Rach established the training restaurant in order to give young people a chance.

Coffee break in the sun at the Oberhafen-Kantine

rant at the other end of the jetty. It's really cosy inside in the winter. *Daily, Nov–Feb Thu–Sun only | Strandweg, Anleger Blankenese | tel. 040 86 64 51 27 | express bus 48 Blankenese/ferry*

SEASON 🕐 (136 B2) (*∅ K5*)
Healthy, fresh, vegetarian – that's their motto. No wonder, after all it is located in the Haus des Sports, the home of the Hamburg Sports Association. During the week breakfast is available from 7am, and there's buffet from midday. Lots of large tables, ideal for gatherings. *Daily | Schäferkampsallee 1 | tel. 040 31 70 62 66 | U 2 Schlump*

SCHWEIZWEIT (135 E4) (*∅ H6*)
This 'Little Switzerland' is located in a basement and in addition to its INSIDER TIP cheese delicacies from the cantons it serves fondue and all kinds of other Swiss specialities. Book in advance! *Daily | Große Rainstr. 20 | tel. 040 39 90 70 00 | bus and S-Bahn Altona*

TH2 (129 E6) (*∅ N3*)
Light, bright and only slightly overpriced. The stylish bistro goes well with the elegant district of Winterhude. Their breakfast served with a good choice of teas is excellent. *Daily | Mühlenkamp 59 | tel. 040 27 88 00 80 | metro bus 6 Goldbekplatz*

TI BREIZH (124 C5) (*∅ L7*)
Pure Brittany with crêpes and cider. In summer they have tables on the pontoon on the Nikolaifleet. They also have a little shop selling Brittany-style fisherman's shirts. *Daily | Deichstr. 39 | tel. 040 37 51 78 15 | U 3 Rödingsmarkt*

INSIDER TIP ZUM STECKELHÖRN (125 D5) (*∅ M7*)
Lunch spot at the edge of the Speicherstadt. No frills, just hearty fare at moderate prices. Host Detlev Block is well connected in the area and will gladly give you tips. Regulars tend to stay in longer to play cards. *Lunch only, closed Sat/Sun | tel. 040 36 65 60 | Steckelhörn 12 | U 1 Meßberg*

SHOPPING

CITY **WHERE TO START?**

Hamburg's main shopping streets, Spitalerstraße and Mönckebergstraße with their department stores near the main station, lead through to the Rathausmarkt. All around the city hall things get more Hanseatic and stylish and you'll find some beautiful traditional shops. From there you can stroll along the flagship addresses of the Große Bleichen or the Neuer Wall towards the Jungfernstieg. *S-/U-Bahn Jungfernstieg*

Shopping in Hamburg is a lot of fun, whether it be in the heart of the city or in the lively surrounding districts.

All around the Jungfernstieg and the Gänsemarkt, in the Hanseviertel and the Hamburger Hof you'll find exclusive haute couture and jewellery shops. The department stores and cheaper shops are located towards the main station. Those who prefer small, quality shops will find what they're looking for along the city's side streets: the Altstädter Straße near the station or around Poolstraße near the Laieszhalle, where bespoke tailors, violin makers and young designers offer their wares for sale.

Photo: Window display at Modehaus Unger on Neuer Wall

A sailor shirt or a designer gown? Hamburg is a shopper's paradise where you can have your every wish fulfilled

Each district has its own shopping area and there are numerous fashion shops along the exclusive Eppendorfer Baum and the Lange Reihe in St Georg, where alongside established businesses, more and more lingerie and label shops are opening up and window-shopping is a lot of fun. And in Ottensen, in the Schanzenviertel and in Winterhude there is an unbelievable variety of fashion boutiques and furnishings

shops, delicatessens and specialist outlets. Closing times are flexible: every shop can stay open as long as it wants, except for Sundays and public holidays; but there are exceptions there as well – at the airport and main railway station. The department stores in the city centre are usually open until 8pm, with smaller shops often closing earlier. On the Reeperbahn shopping can also be done at night.

Funky kitchen utensils: exhibits at the Stilwerk design emporium

DELICATESSEN

BONSCHELADEN (135 D4) (*ш H6*)
Homemade sweets with strawberry, liquorice or ginger flavour; INSIDER TIP exquisite cream caramels, which are made before the customer's eyes. *Closed Mon | Friedensallee 12 | bus and S-Bahn station Altona*

HUMMER PEDERSEN ★
(135 F6) (*ш J7*)
Joachim Niehusen is passionate about seafood, and he passionately sells his lobster and fish, whether in his shop or the pleasant bistro. INSIDER TIP If you arrive before 2pm, then you can admire the fresh daily catch. *Mon–Fri 8am–4pm, Sat until noon, Bistro Mon–Sat 11am–5pm | Große Elbstr. 152 | bus 111 Sandberg*

KAREN'S KONDITOREI (136 B1) (*ш K4*)
Tiny family business, but Hamburg connoisseurs know that this is where you get some of the best cakes and croissants in

the city. *Closed Mon | Beim Schlump 14 | metro bus 5 Bezirksamt Eimsbüttel*

KARSTEN HAGENAH (135 D2) (*ш G4*)
Completely gutted by fire at the end of 2012, business continues in a tent, and soon everything will be back as it was. A huge selection of fresh fish, crab salad and smoked fish to take away and grilled fish in the bistro. *Mon–Wed 7am–4pm, Thu/Fri 7am–6pm, Sat 7am–1pm | Schnackenburgallee 8 | bus 180 Ruhrstraße*

MUTTERLAND (125 F3) (*ш M6*)
Here you can buy German delicacies. The shop and café are located at the main railway station, so it's perfect for travel supplies and souvenirs, such as INSIDER TIP the Kakao Kontor chocolate from Eimsbüttel. A word of caution: they might look really nice but some of the goods are overpriced. *Café also open Sun | Ernst-Merck-Str. 9 | S-/U-Bahn Hauptbahnhof*

K. W. STÜDEMANN (136 A3) (*ш K5*)
Nostalgic shop in the Schanzenviertel. Despite the chichi clientele, the locals still keep coming to this chocolatier for the very best biscuits, tea and coffee. *Schulterblatt 59 | metro bus 15 Schulterblatt*

WEINKAUF ST GEORG (137 E4) (*ш N6*)
The shop's own 'St-Georg' sparkling wine is the bestseller. Schnapps and oil is bottled straight from the carafe. During wine tasting the owners are happy to tell visitors about the district. *Lange Reihe 73 | S-/U-Bahn Hauptbahnhof*

FURNISHINGS ETC.

CUCINARIA (128 B5) (*ш L3*)
This specialist store in Eppendorf has more than 6,000 kitchen items. Homemade Italian specialities are served in the *Cucibar*. *Straßenbahnring 12 | U 3 Hoheluftbrücke*

DIBBERN (124 C3) *(Ⅲ L6)*

An entire shop devoted to fine crockery, tablecloths and glasses from the exclusive North German brand. *Hohe Bleichen 19 | U 2 Gänsemarkt*

HÄNGEMATTENLADEN (135 D5) *(Ⅲ H6)*

The name means 'the hammock shop'. Net hammocks, family-sized hammocks, hanging chairs and even INSIDERTIP hammocks for babies. Not expensive and with competent sales assistants. *Bei der Reitbahn 2 | bus and S-Bahn station Altona*

LOCKENGELÖT (124 A2) *(Ⅲ K6)*

Wonderfully eccentric: toilet roll holders made from vinyl records, a cupboard from oil barrels and coat racks made from old books. Good website, but the shop itself is something to see. *Marktstr. 119 | U 3 Feldstraße*

STILWERK ★ ● (135 F5) *(Ⅲ J7)*

The restored maltings at the Fischmarkt is home to seven floors of exclusive brands, from designer lights to kitchens to upholstered furniture. And even if you don't have the money, window-shopping here can be inspiring. *Sun viewing-only day | Große Elbstr. 68 | bus 111 Fischauktionshalle*

INSIDERTIP DIE WOHNGESCHWISTER (136 A3) *(ⅢK5)*

Lübke senior ran the legendary 'Speicher' at the Fischmarkt. Now his two sons run the shop on the Schanze, while his two daughters continue to design all kinds of practical foam furniture. *Schanzenstr. 34 | S-/U-Bahn Sternschanze*

LOCAL SPECIALITIES

BUDDEL-BINI (129 D4) *(ⅢM2)*

The Binikowski family has sold ships in bottles for more than 30 years, a business that's now run by the second generation.

Good online shop. *Barmbeker Str.171 | www.buddelbini.com | U 1 Hudtwalckerstraße*

ERNST BRENDLER (125 D4) *(ⅢM7)*

Naval and maritime uniforms as well as tropical clothing specialist. The venerable shop has been in business since 1879 and still retains a hint of the colonial era. *Große Johannisstr. 15 | U 3 Rathausmarkt*

WEDE (124 C3) *(ⅢL6)*

Traditional shop for the model enthusiast in the Hanseviertel with more than 1,000 aircraft and ship models on the shelves: from the Harbour Ferry to Queen Mary II; also specialist books and maps. *Große Bleichen 36 | S-/U-Bahn Jungfernstieg*

MARKETS

FLEA MARKETS

In the flea market season there is always a market going on in some district at some time. Check the local papers for info.

★ **Hummer Pedersen**
Seafood can't get any fresher: traditional fishmonger on the Elbe → p. 74

★ **Stilwerk**
Almost too beautiful to buy. Designer goods in the old maltings on the banks of the Elbe → p. 75

★ **Isemarkt**
Germany's longest market, sheltered from the rain under an elevated railway line → p. 76

★ **Globetrotter**
Where just the purchase of equipment is a real adventure → p. 78

MARCO POLO HIGHLIGHTS

MARKETS

WEEKLY MARKETS

Arguably the most attractive but undeniably the longest weekly market in Germany is ★ **Isemarkt** (Tue, Fri 9am–2pm): the fruit, vegetable and cheese stall-holders spread out their wares under the elevated railway line between Hoheluftbrücke and Eppendorfer Baum (U3). A must for those with a sweet tooth is INSIDER TIP **Bonbon Pingel** with biscuits and liquorice for everyone to try. Each district has its own weekly market, with a total of around 100 in Hamburg. Look in the local press for times or at *www.hamburger-wochenmaerkte.de*. And for those who can't get enough during the day: every Wednesday (4pm–11pm, Nov–March until 10pm) there is an atmospheric INSIDER TIP night market that takes place on Spielbudenplatz (Reeperbahn / U 3 St Pauli).

ELEGANT FASHION

LADAGE & OELKE
(125 D4) (*ω L6*)

The traditional local prefers to dress like an Englishman: duffle coat, blazer, muted colours, dignified, discreet. That's exactly what you'll find here where that tradition continues. *Neuer Wall 11 / S-/U-Bahn Jungfernstieg*

POLICKE (137 F4) (*ω N6*)

Here there's no such thing as 'it doesn't suit you'! There's an enormous and reasonably priced choice of mostly classic menswear, and the closely packed rows of suits extend over several floors. *Böckmannstr. 1a / S-/U-Bahn Hauptbahnhof*

WÄSCHEHAUS MÖHRING
(124 C4) (*ω L6*)

In this venerable establishment you will find an impressive selection of linens, nightwear and underwear. Established in the heart of the city for more than 200 years. *Neuer Wall 25 / S-/U-Bahn Jungfernstieg*

C FASHION

ANGELOS (136 A2) (*ω K4*)

Good wearable fashion – for men too. Excellent service. *Weidenstieg 11 / U 2 Christuskirche*

Rainproof market: an elevated railway line shelters the Isemarkt

HARD ROCK CAFÉ
(136 B5) (* 🗺 K7*)
Firstly, you find them in many other cities, secondly it is a popular place to eat, and thirdly they sell their world famous tops, jewellery and accessories. Three good reasons why the place is always packed! *St Pauli Landungsbrücken, Brücke 5 | U- and S-Bahn Landungsbrücken*

HERR VON EDEN
(124 A2) (*🗺 K6*)
Herr von Eden, alias Bent Angelo Jensen, has long supplied distinctive and elegant outfits for fashion-conscious men and women, including Lady Gaga and Depeche Mode. Well known for his stylish and impeccably made bespoke suits. *Markt- str. 33 | U 3 Feldstraße*

WERKHAUS (135 F5) (*🗺 J7*)
Run by a young Dane, this shop right on the Elbe stocks Scandinavian designer labels such as Tiger of Sweden and Linde- berg. *Sun viewing only 1pm–6pm | Große Elbstr. 146 | bus 111 Sandberg*

WIE ES EUCH GEFÄLLT
(136 A3) (*🗺 K5*)
Boutique stocking the imaginative and playful creations of young Hamburg fash- ion designers, from jersey dresses and blouses to jewellery and stylish accessories. *Juliusstr. 16 | S-/U-Bahn Sternschanze*

MUSIC

HANSEPLATTE (136 B4) (*🗺 K6*)
This trendy record shop right next to the old abattoir sells music made by Hamburg-based artists and labels such as Kettcar CDs or Tocotronic, as well as some unusual souvenirs and clothes. Readings and concerts are also held here. *Neuer Kamp 32 | www.hanseplatte.de | U 3 Feldstraße*

JUST MUSIC (136 B4) (*🗺 K6*)
Professionals and amateurs alike can find everything they need in this music shop covering two floors of a bunker on the Heiligengeistfeld, from electric bass and violins to DJ equipment or drumsticks. And you can try out almost every instru- ment – even in the drums department on the first floor. *Feldstr. 66 | in Hochbunker | U 3 Feldstraße*

MICHELLE (125 E4) (*🗺 M6*)
In Hamburg's 'only true' record shop, bands regularly give INSIDER TIP ▶ concerts in the window. Flyers give details about the best gigs in town. *Gertrudenkirchhof 10 | U 3 Mönckebergstraße*

STEINWAY (135 D1) (*🗺 H4*)
The name Steinway has been associated with Hamburg since 1880. Both the piano shop and the factory are now in Bahrenfeld. Concerts are held in Steinway's own con- cert hall. *Rondenbarg 15 | www.steinway- hamburg.de | S 3, 21 Diebsteich | bus 180 Marlowring*

SHOPPING ARCADES

● Believe it or not there are 13 shopping arcades in central Hamburg. Theoretically you could shop all day between Gänse- markt and Hauptbahnhof (main railway station) without feeling a single drop of rain or gust of wind. The *Europa-Passage* (125 D4) (*🗺 M6*), designed by Hamburg's favourite architect Hadi Teherani, is the largest shopping mall in the city. It is a five-storey palace of consumerism (from the top you have a superb view over the Binnenalster) with glass lifts, shops, fast food outlets and even an art gallery displaying works by Germany's aging rocker Udo Lindenberg. Whether for people watching or more exclusive shopping, the locals also like going to *Galleria* (124 C4) (*🗺 L6*), where a French bistro serves café au lait or champagne to go with the nice view over the canal. Architects also succeeded in converting the *Levantehaus* (125 E4) (*Ø M6*), a 100-year-old *Kontorhaus* office building on Mönckebergstraße, into a chic shopping arcade where shops invite you to browse and window-shop.

SHOES & BAGS

FREITAG (125 F4) (*Ø M7*)
The trendy Swiss cult label stocks original bags made from recycled truck tarpaulins. *Klosterwall 9 | S-/U-Bahn Hauptbahnhof*

INGA THOMAS MODELLSCHUHE (124 A2) (*Ø K6*)
Shoes without a trace of leather! The young designer creates her super-chic specimens from hi-tech materials and

LOW BUDGET

▶ At the *Flohschanze* flea market (136 B4) (*Ø K6*) *(Sat 9am–4pm | Neuer Kamp 30 | U 3 Feldstraße)* you can find almost everything from old rags to oil paintings – and extremely cheaply at that.

▶ *Secondella* (124 C3) (*Ø L6*) *(Hohe Bleichen 5 | S 1, 3 Stadthausbrücke)* is *the* place to go for quirky second-hand designer clothes, for the kids too.

▶ The cards of Hamburg filled with tea from *Tee-Maass* (125 D4) (*Ø M7*) *(Börsenbrücke 2 a | U 3 Rathaus)* make an unusual souvenir. The well-established shop also sells nice crockery and Hanseatic tea blends at reasonable prices.

takes measurements on the spot. The finished articles are sent out by post. *Mon–Sat from noon | Marktstr. 119 | U 3 Feldstraße*

KLOCKMANN (124 C3) (*Ø L6*)
One hundred years ago Ernst Klockmann began designing cases. If you have some money left over, do consider having a INSIDERTIP 'Hamburger Beutel' (Hamburg bag) made, finished off to your own specifications – with magnetic snap or zip closure and lining of your choice. *Gänsemarkt 50 | Gänsemarktpassage | U 2 Gänsemarkt*

SCHUH MESSMER (136 A5) (*Ø K7*)
The oldest shoe store in the city now offers shoes with some very high heels. Men come here for their snakeskin ankle boots and thigh high boots that are available in extra large shoe sizes. *Also Sun 2pm–8pm | Reeperbahn 77 | S 1, 3 Reeperbahn*

SPECIALIST SHOPS

FAHNEN FLECK (124 C4) (*Ø L6*)
This shop is as much a part of Hamburg as St Michael's church tower: carnival costumes, masks, fireworks and the full range of national flags. *Neuer Wall 57 | S-/U-Bahn Jungfernstieg*

GLOBETROTTER ★ (130 B5) (*Ø P3*)
The more exotic the destination and mode of travel, the more attentive the service: this magnet for all outdoor enthusiasts is located in a bright red cube at Barmbek station. There's a climbing wall and a walk-in refrigerator for testing specialist equipment. *Wiesendamm 1 | S-/U-Bahn Barmbek*

GUTE JACKE (125 E6) (*Ø M7*)
You might not think it, but HafenCity has some nice little independent shops. This

one sells jackets for your walk along the Elbe or your next visit to the Alps. Good service. *Überseeboulevard 3 | U 4 Übersee-quartier*

MÄRKLIN STORE
(125 E4) (*M6*)

Model railway fans will love the ground floor of the Levantehaus where engines, goods and high-speed trains exclusively from this high-quality brand are on show. *Mönckebergstr. 7, S-/U-Bahn Hauptbahnhof*

MEISTER PARFÜMERIE
(128 C6) (*L3*)

Unusual scents for refined senses! A genuinely beautiful shop, which has re-mained in family ownership since 1888. *Eppendorfer Baum 12 | U 1 Klosterstern*

NIVEA HAUS (125 D3) (*L6*)

Nivea comes from Hamburg – so what could be more appropriate than one of the blue tins as a souvenir? Or treat your-self to a massage in the spa (from 80 euros). *Jungfernstieg 51 | tel. appointment 040 82 22 47 40 | S-/U-Bahn Jungfernstieg*

PAPPNASE & CO (136 C2) (*L5*)

Enough to make anyone smile: balls for juggling, red noses, complete clown out-fits and makeup; a comic shop with pub-lications from around the world can be found next door. *Grindelallee 92 | metro bus 4, 5 Grindelhof*

SCHIRM & CO (125 E4) (*M6*)

This umbrella shop is a Hamburg institu-tion and they are also open longer on rainy days. The Vertein family also pro-vides a repair service for broken umbrel-las. *Rosenstr. 6 | S-/U-Bahn Hauptbahnhof*

STEGMANN (125 D3) (*L6*)

At one time this was Germany's only spe-cialist shop for buttons, but these have

Shopping under cover: Europa-Passage

since been supplemented by ladies' cloth-ing, scarves and other accessories. *Jung-fernstieg 46 | U 2 Gänsemarkt*

STEIFF GALERIE
(125 E4) (*M6*)

Soft toys everywhere: these much-loved animals with their distinctive ear tags are piled up high on the shelves. An absolute paradise for the young and the young at heart. *Mönckebergstr. 7 (in the Levante-haus) | S-/U-Bahn Hauptbahnhof*

THE ART OF HAMBURG
(124 A5) (*K7*)

The 'Machinist' T-shirts with real oil stains (not guaranteed to come out) have cult status and are a tribute to the nearby port, as are the hoodies with maritime logos. All around the side streets of the Portuguese district you can find other nice shops. *Ditmar-Koel-Str. 19 | S-/U-Bahn Landungs-brücken*

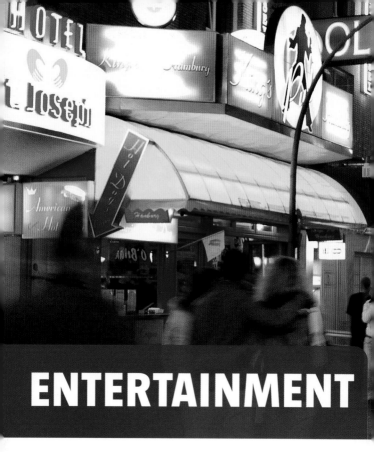

ENTERTAINMENT

WHERE TO START?

CITY
Nightfall in Hamburg: it's always the **Reeperbahn (136 A5)** (*[ill]* *J–K 7*) that comes to mind. It is where the best clubs and bars are, and it's also just a stone's throw from the other trendy area of the Schanzenviertel. It's simply *the* place to go. Even culturally minded people are well catered for: from musicals to theatre to cabaret. If it's too crowded for you and you'd just prefer a leisurely beer, almost all districts of the city have their own nightlife.

First the good news: Hamburg's nightlife is easy to get the hang of. St Pauli, the Schanzenviertel, Ottensen and St Georg – the real revellers' hotspots – can readily be navigated by public transport.

But that's about as far as the prescription for a good night out can go, simply because the scene is so varied. St Pauli has the important live music clubs, the trendy bars and discos, cheek by jowl with dimly lit pubs and amusement arcades. A new place opens up somewhere almost every week. Go with the flow, be curious and visit places where the atmosphere looks good, such as around Hans-Albers-Platz for example. There you'll find young people,

Photo: Große Freiheit, a side street off the Reeperbahn

The main entertainment area is the Reeperbahn – but there's plenty of nightlife in other parts of the city as well

Hanseatics and tourists all drinking and dancing. In the summertime the Elbe beach between Neumühlen and Teufelsbrück is one big open-air pub. They barbecue and chill out and the restaurants and bars are all packed. Ottensen has more pubs than clubs, and here too on warm summer evenings you sit outside, even if it's just with a can bought from the local kiosk. In the Schanzenviertel, as well as the lively bar scene along the Schulterblatt you have the option of smarter and quieter bars. The Lange Reihe in St Georg is where touts, theatregoers and the established gay scene congregate. Out towards Steindamm prostitution and drug dealing represent the seamier side of the city's nightlife. HafenCity is one district that has not yet developed any real nightlife of its own: there are cafés but that's about it.

Die Bank: popular with the chic crowd

Hamburg offers an exciting cultural and theatre scene, and is even slowly developing a genuine fringe scene *(www.hamburg-off.de)*. The Hamburg Staatsoper (opera house), the Schauspielhaus (theatre) and Thalia Theater are among the leading such institutions in the country. But the Hamburg audience is considered a critical one; new directors must first prove themselves before they are embraced. Premieres and musicals are often sold out. To see highlights such as John Neumeier's 'Ballet Days' fans will literally camp out in front of the ticket office. If you'd like to see a performance it's best to book in advance. You'll find what's on and when in the newspapers, online and in various magazines; tickets are also available through the *Hamburg Tourism* hotline (→ p. 113).

BARS & CAFÉS

Unless otherwise stated, the city's trendy cafés are open every day from 10 or 11am. Most of them offer breakfast, and often brunch on Sundays. As a rule the bars and clubs only open up in the evenings. They close once the last people have left.

AUREL (135 D4) *(Ø H6)*
A good place to start or finish your night out in Ottensen. It's very full in the summer and the pavement serves as an extension to the bar. It's no less popular in winter and quite a cosy squeeze inside. *Daily | Bahrenfelder Str. 157 | tel. 040 3 90 27 27 | bus and S-Bahn Altona*

DIE BANK (124 C3) *(Ø L6)*
Brasserie and bar located in an old bank – stunning interior and hotspot for the chic set. *Closed Sun | Hohe Bleichen 17 | tel. 040 2 38 00 30 | U 2 Gänsemarkt*

CIU ☆ (125 E3) *(Ø M6)*
In summer you're spoiled for choice between the chic bar indoors and the smart benches outside – if you sit outside you're more likely to be noticed and that's what it's all about – quite a wanna-be crowd. *Daily from 4pm, Sun from 6pm | Ballindamm 14–15 | tel. 040 32 52 60 60 | S-/U-Bahn Jungfernstieg*

GOLEM (135 F5) *(Ø J7)*
This bar at the Fischmarkt attracts the in-crowd even in the depths of winter with

its classic cocktails, old piano and trendy party nights. If you prefer edgy, go a few doors further on to the live rock club *Hafenklang. Wed–Sun from 8pm (weekends from 10pm with admission) | Große Elbstr. 14 | bus 111 Fischauktionshalle*

PIANO BEACH ⚖ (135 D6) (*∅ H7*)

Fine sand, sunshades, sun loungers, and a drink at the miniature pool while looking out at the passing ships – at the posh beach club in Neumühlen the magnificent view of the port and Elbe is free. *15 April–15 Sept, Mon–Fri from 3pm, Sat/Sun from noon | Neumühlen 11 | tel. 040 39 80 78 80 | bus 111, 112 Neumühler Kirchenweg*

INSIDER TIP STRANDPAULI
(136 A5) (*∅ K7*)

There are a few beach clubs in Hamburg but this is the nicest, firmly established alongside the shipping piers. Don't miss the tango evenings on the terrace. *April–Sept | St Pauli Hafenstr. 89 | S-/U-Bahn Landungsbrücken*

20 UP LOUNGE & BAR ★ ⚖
(136 A5) (*∅ K7*)

Fabulous views: the bar overlooks Hamburg from the 20th floor of the *Empire Riverside Hotel*. The people of Hamburg love to show their guests this view of their city so the place is busy, and there is a dress code. *Daily from 6pm | Bernhard-Nocht-Str. 97 | tel. 040 31 11 97 04 70 | S-/U-Bahn Landungsbrücken*

CLUBS & DISCOS

ANGIE'S NIGHTCLUB (136 A5) (*∅ K7*)
A neighbourhood perennial that has live music every evening – either from Angie's house band or invited guests. INSIDER TIP Good danceable soul, funk and pop. *Thu–Sat from 10pm | 10 euros (Thu 5 euros) | Spielbudenplatz 27 | tel. 040 31 77*

88 11 | www.angies-nightclub.de | S 1, 3 Reeperbahn*

CHINA LOUNGE (136 A5) (*∅ J7*)

A word of caution: this place is often bursting at the seams and things only calm down after 2 or 3am – this club has been one of the area's top nightlife addresses for years. *Usually Thu–Sat from 11pm | from 8 euros | Nobistor 14 | tel. 040 31 97 66 22 | www.china-hamburg.de | S 1, 3 Reeperbahn*

FRAU HEDI (136 A6) (*∅ K7*)

A different kind of harbour tour: in summer the INSIDER TIP party boat 'Frau Hedi' cruises around the harbour, and the passengers chill out and dance. *April–Oct*

★ **Mojo Club**
The Mojo is back, so you can dance the night away → p. 84

★ **20 up Lounge & Bar**
Even the cool in-crowd gets excited by the breathtaking a view! → p. 83

★ **Uebel & Gefährlich**
The scene is alive and well: dancing in an old bunker → p. 87

★ **Schmidt-Theater**
Cult status venue with glamour, show and song → p. 88

★ **Staatsoper/Hamburg Ballet**
Two cultural treasures of the Hanseatic city → p. 89

★ **Thalia Theater**
A class act: the finest theatre in town → p. 89

MARCO POLO HIGHLIGHTS

CLUBS & DISCOS

Mon–Fri from 7pm, Sat/Sun from 6pm hourly, variable in winter | 6–9 euros | Landungsbrücke 10 | Innenkante | www. frauhedi.de | S-/U-Bahn Landungsbrücken

GOLDEN PUDEL CLUB
(136 A5) (*ɰ K7*)

The club of the multi-talented artist Rocko Schamoni is the place to go if you want to see the sunrise over the port. Getting a bit shabby and the upstairs café above is not exactly eye-catching but music fans don't let that bother them. *Daily from around 10pm, café from noon | St.-Pauli-Fischmarkt 27 | tel. 040 31 97 99 30 | www. pudel.com | S-/U-Bahn Landungsbrücken*

KULTURHAUS III & 70
(136 A3) (*ɰ K5*)

Whether theatre, song-writer slams, political debates or watching football, there's something going on every day in this culture club in the 'Schanze'. Frequented by teenies and twenty-somethings at weekends; very popular with local bohemians during the week. *Daily | Schulterblatt 73 | tel. 040 3 19 75 55 12 | www.drei undsiebzig.de | metro bus 15 Schulterblatt*

MOJO CLUB ★ (136 B5) (*ɰ K7*)

The years when Mojo was closed are already forgotten. The new location beneath the 'Dancing Towers' is unfortunately a bit too cool but the music is just as it used to be: excellent! *Several live concerts per week | prices and times vary | Reeperbahn 1 | www.mojo.de | U 3 St Pauli*

OLIVIAS WILDE JUNGS
(136 A5) (*ɰ J6*)

Germany's only male strip joint, for women only. Gogo boys and an hourly strip dance

CITY OF SPORT? ABSOLUTELY!

Hamburg never got to host the Olympic Games, but the locals are still mad about their sport. Every year in April half the city turns out for the *Marathon (www.haspa-marathon-hamburg.de/index.php/en)*. They cheer along and clap or they participate. The city also goes crazy for the *Hamburg Triathlon (one weekend in July | www.hamburg-triathlon.org/en/home)*. The most important streets are closed to traffic and anyone who wants to can take part in the 'Jedermann' – and you shouldn't miss out on the chance of swimming the Alster just once! The professionals then demonstrate how it's really done. The *Cyclassics (www. vattenfall-cyclassics.de/index.php/en)* is another major event that takes place in August: the cycling race goes right through the city and amateurs follow the professionals – a massive event.

Those who prefer being a spectator go to the football (→ p. 21) or to O₂ World (formerly the Color Line Arena). That's where the Hamburg Freezers ice hockey team is based; the games are always very entertaining *(season Sept–March | tickets from 21 euros | ticket hotline: 01805 20 84 08 (*) | www.hamburg-freezers.de)*. Another interesting sports options is watching the HSV handball team, who were German champions in 2011 *(O₂ World | season Sept–June | tickets from 14.50 euros | ticket hotline: tel. 01805 9 69 00 06 66 (*) | www. hsvhandball.com)*.

when the crowd goes wild – what more could a woman want? *Thu/Fri from 8.30pm, Sat from 8pm (closed Jan, Feb/March, Nov/Dec Fri/Sat only) | admission 10 euros | Große Freiheit 32 | www.olivia-jones.de | S 1, 3 Reeperbahn*

INSIDER TIP QUEEN CALAVERA
(136 A5) (*∅ K7*)

Queen Calavera is a burlesque club where the staff dress in 1920s style, and the dancers perform on a mini stage. The erotic striptease never reveals all: but at least the ladies still have female curves. There is even enough room for a DJ and a dance floor. *18 and over | Thu from 8pm, Fri/Sat from 9pm, show every 30 minutes until 3am | admission 5 euros | Gerhardstr. 7 | www.queencalavera.com | S 1, 3 Reeperbahn*

CINEMAS

ABATON (136 C2) (*∅ L5*)
Hamburg's nicest and one of the best art house cinemas in Europe. Afterwards you can discuss the movie in the INSIDER TIP *Abaton Bistro. Allende-Platz 3 | tel. 040 41 32 03 20 | www.abaton.de | metro bus 4, 5 Grindelhof*

METROPOLIS (124 C3) (*∅ L6*)
This cinema next to the opera house shows silent movies with piano or orchestral accompaniment. The place has recently been modernised but the artistic standards with great movie specials remain unchanged. *Kleine Theaterstr. 10 | tel. 040 34 23 53 | www.metropoliskino.de | U 1 Stephansplatz*

ZEISE KINOS (135 D4) (*∅ H6*)
Good films (no blockbusters) are shown in the old propeller factory in Ottensen. *Friedensallee 9 | tel. 040 3 90 87 70 | www.zeise.de | metro bus 2 Friedensallee*

Borchers is a traditional pub in Eppendorf

PUBS & WINE BARS

BORCHERS (128 C4) (*∅ L2*)
Borchers has been *the* pub in Eppendorf ever since 1906. Pleasant beer garden under the trees, dance night every third Saturday in the month, Sunday brunch. *Daily | Geschwister-Scholl-Str. 1 | tel. 040 46 26 77 | metro bus 20, 22, 25 Eppendorfer Marktplatz*

FC ST PAULI CLUBHEIM
(136 B4) (*∅ K6*)

In the heart of the district is the FC St Pauli football stadium; the clubhouse is a public bar, with all the games shown live on a big screen. Beer garden open in the summer. *Mon–Thu from noon, Fri from 7pm, Sat/Sun open for home games and Bundesliga highlights | Heiligengeistfeld | tel. 040 31 78 74 95 | U 3 St Pauli*

FRAU MÖLLER (137 E4) (*ØJ N6*)
The Lange Reihe in the St Georg district used to be one of the most colourful streets in Hamburg. Now it's been gentrified and only a few islands remain, including this lovely pub (with good food and eight varieties of draught beer). Local residents, actors from the nearby playhouse, hotel staff and of course visitors from out of town all gather here. *Daily | Lange Reihe 96 | tel. 040 25 32 88 17 | metro bus 6 Gurlittstraße*

LANDHAUS WALTER (129 E4) (*ØJ N2*)
This isn't just the location of Hamburg's only real beer garden (in the park), but also live concerts and the 'Downtown Bluesclub', where the over 40s generation can also enjoy themselves. *Daily (Oct–March closed Mon) | Hindenburgstr. 2 | tel. 040 27 50 54 | www.landhauswalter. de | U 3 Borgweg*

SAAL II
(136 A3) (*ØJ K5*)
The Saal bar is a lively, yet at the same time relaxed, venue near the *Rote Flora* and the busy bars of the Schanzenviertel on the piazza opposite. *Daily | Schulterblatt 83 | tel. 040 4 39 28 28 | S-/U-Bahn Sternschanze*

INSIDER TIP **SCHELLFISCHPOSTEN**
(135 F5) (*ØJ J7*)
The old seaman's pub at the Fischmarkt has been enjoying a renaissance ever since a late-night TV show started being broadcast from here. *Daily | Carsten-Rehder-Str. 62 | tel. 040 38 34 22 | bus 111 Fischauktionshalle*

LOW BUDGET

▶ Communal telly on Sunday and lots of music during the week, including live jazz every Wednesday, is supplied free of charge at the *Pony Bar* **(136 C2)** (*ØJ L5*) (*Allende-Platz 1 | www.ponybar.com | metro bus 4, 5 Grindelhof*)

▶ Enjoy good party music for free at the *Sommersalon* **(136 A5)** (*ØJ K7*) (*daily from 6pm, from 7pm in winter | Spielbudenplatz 22 | www.sommer salon.de | S 1, 3 Reeperbahn*).

▶ World-class opera and ballet performances **(124 C3)** (*ØJ L6*) (→ p. 88), and they're affordable, with tickets available from 10 euros.

▶ Hamburg's churches are wonderful venues for classical concerts, with or without a choir. Sometimes there are bargains to be had. Information: *www.kirchenmusik-nordelbien.de*.

LIVE MUSIC

FABRIK
(135 D4) (*ØJ H6*)
Well-established venue in Altona; some bands have been performing here for decades. It doesn't have the best acoustics but the atmosphere makes up for that. Saturday night is often party night. *Barnerstr. 36 | tel. 040 39 10 70 | www.fabrik.de | bus and S-Bahn Altona*

FREILICHTBÜHNE IM STADTPARK
(130 A3) (*ØJ O2*)
Concerts at the open-air stage go ahead regardless of Hamburg's summer showers. Many local bands perform in the green Stadtpark (city park), as well as really international acts such as Crosby, Stills & Nash. *Ticket hotline: 040 4 13 22 60 | www.open-r.de | S 1 Alte Wöhr*

KNUST (136 B4) (*K6*)

At its new home in the old abattoir, this club, which was once an infamous dive, has become an established concert venue. *Neuer Kamp 30 | www.knusthamburg.de | U 3 Feldstraße*

O₂ WORLD (126 B–C5) (*F3*)

This 16,000-seat venue puts on anything that draws the crowds. It's where the likes of Eric Clapton, Dieter Nuhr and Alicia Keys perform, but it also stages sports events: handball, ice hockey and boxing. *Sylvesterallee 10 | ticket hotline: 040 80 60 20 80 | www.o2world-hamburg. de | S 3, 21 Stellingen | shuttle buses for performances/events*

UEBEL & GEFÄHRLICH ★
(136 B4) (*K6*)

Sub-culture and mainstream – this venue has gained quite a reputation for its live music and party nights, which are very popular. International bands are pretty taken with the location – the 4th floor of a World War II bunker! The lift even has an attendant during performances. *Usually Wed–Sat from 8pm and according to the programme; parties from midnight | Feldstr. 66 | Medienbunker | www.uebel undgefaehrlich.com | U 3 Feldstraße*

ZWICK ALTONA (135 E4) (*J6*)

Rock 'n roll restaurant and bar with football simulcasts. Smoking is permitted. So what are you waiting for boys and girls, get your leathers out! *Max-Brauer-Allee 86 | tel. 040 57 22 57 11 | www.zwick4u.com | bus 15, 20, 25 Gerichtsstraße*

Fabrik in Ottensen: a landmark for live music fans

MUSICALS

Hamburg is the musical capital of Germany, soon to have four music theatres. All the musicals performed here are laid on by Stage Entertainment and run from Thu–Sun. Central ticket reservation: *tel. 01805 44 44 (*)*, online ticket sales: *www.stage-entertainment.de*. Tickets from 39.90 euros.

DER KÖNIG DER LÖWEN
(136 B6) (*K7*)

Disney's Lion King has long become a classic. The African tale dazzles with its amazing masks and costumes. A ferry will take you from the shipping piers to the opposite bank of the Elbe. *Theater im Hafen | Norderelbstraße 6 | S-/U-Bahn Landungsbrücken*

DAS PHANTOM DER OPER
(135 F3) (*J5*)

The Neue Flora opened with a performance of the 'Phantom of the Opera' in 1990. Now the show featuring Andrew Lloyd Webber's music has returned to Hamburg. *Stresemannstraße 163a | S 11, 21, 31 Holstenstraße*

SHOWS & CABARET

ROCKY (136 B5) (⊯ K7)

Nifty stage hydraulics: for the boxing epic (Sylvester Stallone and the Klitschko-brothers co-produce) the foundations of the TUI-Operettenhaus had to be strengthened. *Spielbudenplatz 1 | U 3 St Pauli*

SHOWS & CABARET

DAS SCHIFF (125 C5) (⊯ L7)

Top-class satirists entertain you on this cultural steamer. In summer, Europe's only seaworthy theatre ship casts off and takes guest performances along the Elbe. *Tickets from 20 euros | Holzbrücke 2/Nikolaifleet | tel. 040 69 65 05 60 | www.theaterschiff.de | U 3 Rödingsmarkt*

INSIDER TIP ▶ NACHTASYL
(125 E4) (⊯ M6)

Culture in the attic: this bar is situated on the top floor of the Thalia Theatre, and is used as an experimental stage for young directors and actors. Witty and subtle pieces are premiered here, and it is also a venue for readings, guest concerts and parties. Even when there is nothing going on *(admission 5–20 euros)* the bar, with its reasonable prices, is a nice place to enjoy a glass of wine (no lift, 101 steps). *Daily from 7pm | Alstertor 1 | tel. 040 32 81 44 44 | www.thalia-theater.de | S-/U-Bahn Jungfernstieg*

POLITTBÜRO (137 E4) (⊯ N6)

Biting left-wing satire in St Georg: the frontwoman Lisa Politt has made the former cinema a permanent fixture of Hamburg's cabaret scene. *Tickets 15 euros, reduced rate 10 euros | Steindamm 45 | tel. 040 28 05 54 67 | www.polittbuero.de | U 1 Lohmühlenstraße*

SCHMIDT-THEATER ★
(136 A5) (⊯ K7)

The former president of St Pauli FC, Corny Littmann, is *the* Impresario for the Reeperbahn; both his two venues *(Schmidt-Theater, Schmidts Tivoli)* are cult institutions and never fail to surprise with their witty repertoires. There are also perennial favourites like 'Defending the Caveman' or the 'Midnight Show'. *Spielbudenplatz 24 | tel. 040 31 77 88 99 | www.tivoli.de | S 1, 3 Reeperbahn*

Guaranteed a fun place for a night out: the Schmidt-Theater on Spielbudenplatz

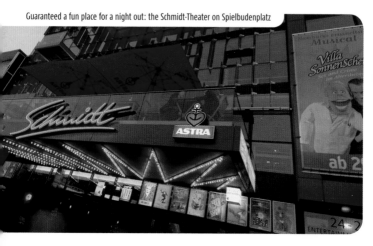

OPERA & CLASSICAL MUSIC

HAMBURG STATE OPERA/HAMBURG BALLET ⭐ (124 C3) (*Ø L6*)

The Australian Simone Young directs the opera, while American John Neumeier looks after the ballet. Both are firmly established in Hamburg and are themselves stars of the local cultural scene. *Dammtorstr. 28 | tel. 040 35 68 68 | www.staatsoper-hamburg.de | www.hamburgballett.de | U 1 Stephansplatz*

LAEISZHALLE (124 B3) (*Ø L6*)

The Laeiszhalle will remain the city's concert house until the new Elbphilharmonie opens its doors. Internationally renowned soloists and orchestras perform here and it is also the home of the Hamburg Symphony Orchestra and the North German Radio Symphony Orchestra. *Johannes-Brahms-Platz | tel. 040 35 76 66 66 | www.laeiszhalle.de | metro bus 3 | bus 112 Johannes-Brahms-Platz*

CASINO

CASINO ESPLANADE (125 D2) (*Ø L6*)

The magnificent white building on the Esplanade is the perfect setting for you to try your luck. There are gaming machines in the hall *(daily from noon)*; in the casino itself the stakes are higher. *Daily from 3pm | admission 2 euros (ID required) | Stephansplatz 10 | tel. 040 3 34 73 30 | www.spielbank-hamburg.de | U 1 Stephansplatz*

THEATRE

DEUTSCHES SCHAUSPIELHAUS (125 F3) (*Ø M6*)

With Karin Beier as its director, this is the first time Germany's largest theatre has a woman at the helm: new horizons lie ahead. The performances in the

INSIDER TIP Junges Schauspielhaus (youth theatre) in the Malersaal are very popular among children and teenagers. *Kirchenallee 39–41 | tel. 040 24 87 13 | www.schauspielhaus.de | S-/U-Bahn Hauptbahnhof*

KAMPNAGELFABRIK (129 F5–6) (*Ø N3*)

Here we have dance and experimental theatre of the highest standard on the premises of an old engineering company; first-rate programme and fantastic **INSIDER TIP** international summer festival in August. Tip: the *Tanznagel* parties on Friday (11pm). *Jarrestr. 20–24 | tel. 040 27 09 49 49 | www.kampnagel.de | bus 172, 173 Jarrestraße*

OHNSORG THEATER (125 F3) (*Ø M6*)

This is only for those who can understand the Low German dialect – then you are in for a lot of down-to-earth fun. *Heidi-Kabel-Platz 1 | tel. 040 35 08 03 21 | www.ohnsorg.de | S-/U-Bahn Hauptbahnhof*

ST PAULI THEATER (136 A5) (*Ø K7*)

Neighbourhood theatre with a long tradition and varied programme. *Spielbudenplatz 29/30 | tel. 040 47 11 06 66 | www.st-pauli-theater.de | U 3 St Pauli*

THALIA THEATER ⭐ (125 E4) (*Ø M6*)

The finest theatre in town, with a permanent star-studded company, a very active director in Joachim Lux and several venues in the main building on Gerhart-Hauptmann-Platz and on Gaußstraße in Ottensen. *Alstertor 1 | tel. 040 32 81 44 44 | www.thalia-theater.de | S-/U-Bahn Jungfernstieg*

WINTERHUDER FÄHRHAUS (129 D4) (*Ø M2*)

The most successful privately owned German comedy theatre. *Hudtwalckerstraße 13 | tel. 040 48 06 80 80 | www.komoedie-hamburg.de | U 1 Hudtwalckerstraße*

WHERE TO STAY

Hotel beds in Hamburg are plentiful. All major chains are represented in the city. Or perhaps you'd prefer a family-run hotel in one of the beautiful villas, or even a night on a ship? Be inspired!

There are more than 300 hotels and guest houses in Hamburg, and the number is on the rise. In HafenCity four or five new hotels are set to open. It's worth looking around and taking into consideration the location: places of interest in Hamburg can be quite far apart. Apart from the major chains there are some wonderful, family-run places that are often not that much more expensive. Events such as the anniversary of the port or a visit by the 'Queen

Mary' push the prices up quite a bit, as do trade fairs. The centrally located hotels are generally fully booked at such times – so book well in advance. Cheap weekend rates and a variety of package deals are available through the *Hamburg Tourist Office (www.hamburg-travel.com)* as part of the 'Happy Hamburg' programme. Cheap combination deals are often available.

HOTELS: EXPENSIVE

EAST (136 A5) *(⌘ K6)*

Designer hotel in a converted steel foundry in St Pauli with beds (also waterbeds) in the middle of the room and bathrooms simply

A bunk, a luxury suite or a waterbed in a designer hotel – there's a variety of ways to spend the night in Hamburg

curtained off. Popular restaurant and bar. *128 rooms | Simon-von-Utrecht-Str. 31 | tel. 040 30 99 30 | www.east-hamburg.de | U 3 St Pauli*

GRAND ELYSÉE (125 D1) *(ωℓ L5)*
Hamburg's Steakhouse king, Eugen Block, has built a monument to himself with the Grand Elysée, which includes Hamburg's biggest ballroom. Non-residents are wel-

come to use the ● spa facilities. Hamburgers like to meet for an afternoon coffee in the lobby. *511 rooms | Rothenbaumchaussee 10 | tel. 040 41 41 20 | www.grand-elysee.com/en | S 21, 31 Dammtor*

PRIVATHOTEL LINDTNER
(142 C4) *(ωℓ O)*
The Lindtner was always a good recommendation, even before anyone started

The Royal Méridien Hotel's stylish Opus Lounge

talking about the 'leap across the Elbe'. Now Harburg is getting ever closer to the city centre, and the hotel, which stands in the middle of a small park, is getting more and more popular. And because space isn't a problem here there is also free parking. *128 rooms | Heimfelder Str. 123 | tel. 040 79 00 90 | www.lindtner.com | bus 142 Heimfelder Straße*

MÖVENPICK HOTEL HAMBURG
(136 B3) (*∅ K5*)

Spectacularly designed: spend the night within the thick walls of the second-tallest water tower in Europe and enjoy the view from the windows over the trade fair grounds. Situated in bohemian Schanzenpark, the project was bitterly fought over for a number of years. *226 rooms | Sternschanze 6 | tel. 040 3 34 41 10 | www.moevenpick-hotels.com | S-/U-Bahn Sternschanze*

PARK HYATT (125 F4) (*∅ M6*)

This hotel is famous for its comfortable beds, a fact also appreciated by the many famous names that have stayed the night in the converted *kontorhaus*. The peaceful lobby on the first floor with its view over the bustling Mönckebergstraße is often used for business meetings. *252 rooms, 30 apartments | Bugenhagenstr. 8–10 | tel. 040 33 32 12 34 | www.hamburg.park. hyatt.com | S-/U-Bahn Hauptbahnhof*

LE ROYAL MÉRIDIEN ⚜
(137 E3) (*∅ N6*)

A gleaming glass façade outside, bright colours and a warm light inside. The exterior glass elevator whisks guests up to the conference rooms and the *Le Ciel* restaurant from where there's a great view over the city. *284 rooms | An der Alster 52–56 | tel. 040 2 10 00 | www.leroyalmeridien hamburg.com | metro bus 6 Gurlittstraße*

SIDE (124 C3) (*∅ L6*)

Even the way to the WC is an object lesson for students of design. The American theatre director Robert Wilson did the lighting in an interior dominated by wood and clean lines. In the *Meatery* restaurant, carnivores can really indulge their passion: steaks at their best! *178 rooms | Drehbahn 49 | tel. 040 30 99 90 | www.side-hamburg.de/en/side-home.html | U 1 Stephansplatz*

STEIGENBERGER HAMBURG
(124 C4) (*ш L7*)

Luxury hotel on the Fleetinsel (canal island) with its own quay – that's Hanseatic style. The ◯ Shiseido Day Spa on the 5th floor has a lovely view over the Elbe. *233 rooms | Heiligengeistbrücke 4 | tel. 040 36 80 60 | www.steigenberger.com/en/Hamburg | S 1, 3 Stadthausbrücke*

HOTELS: MODERATE

HOTEL ALSTER-HOF
(125 D2) (*ш L6*)

Good news for pet owners – INSIDER TIP dogs are welcome here. The hotel is close to the Außenalster, a popular place for dog walkers. Don't forget their blanket. *113 rooms | Esplanade 12 | tel. 040 35 00 70 | www.alster-hof.de | U 1 Stephansplatz*

ALTE WACHE (137 E4) (*ш N6*)
Elegant hotel situated next to the railway station and ideal for those who like to be central. Internet terminals in the lobby. *100 rooms | Adenauerallee 21 | tel. 040 2 84 06 60 | www.hotel-alte-wache.de | S-/U-Bahn Hauptbahnhof*

ASPRIA (137 E1) (*ш N4*)
It can hardly get more chic than this: luxury sport club with pools, garden, saunas, equipment and wonderful fitness trainers, with really generously proportioned hotel rooms to boot. Everything's included, just like the well-heeled guests here on the Uhlenhorst. *48 rooms | Hofweg 40 | tel. 040 8 99 55 01 10 | www.aspriahotels.com/de/hamburg | metro bus 6 Averhoffstraße*

BASELER HOF ⭐ (125 D2) (*ш L6*)
Tradition meets warm hospitality in this centrally located hotel that belongs to the Association of Christian Hotels (VCH). The pleasant hotel restaurant, the *Kleinhuis*, has an acclaimed wine cellar. *167 rooms | Esplanade 11 | tel. 040 35 90 60 | www.baselerhof.de | U 1 Stephansplatz*

EILENAU ⭐ (138 B2) (*ш O5*)
Hamburg's smallest 4-star hotel is idyllically situated on a canal at the edge of the Uhlenhorst district in two beautifully renovated art nouveau villas. It is privately run

---

MARCO POLO HIGHLIGHTS

⭐ **25h Hafencity**
Well-thought through from the bare concrete wall to the cuddly sheep on the bunks → p. 96

⭐ **Baseler Hof**
Centrally located, friendly and steeped in tradition – a really beautiful hotel → p. 93

⭐ **Eilenau**
Hamburg's smallest 4-star hotel near the Außenalster lake → p. 93

⭐ **Henri**
Stylish living in a superbly converted *Kontorhaus* office building in the city → p. 99

⭐ **Fairmont Hotel Vier Jahreszeiten**
One of the world's finest hotels → p. 94

⭐ **Jugendherberge Auf dem Stintfang**
A hostel with the best (and cheapest) view → p. 97

and all rooms are nicely appointed. Very small but really nice! *17 rooms | Eilenau 36–37 | tel. 040 2 36 01 30 | www.eilenau.de | U 3 Uhlandstraße*

GASTWERK HOTEL (135 D3) (*ℳ G5*)
Made of lots of glass and brick, this building in the Otto-von-Bahren-Park, in the rather unattractive district of Bahrenfeld, was among the first designer hotels in the city. An enormous gasworks once stood on the site, today there are flats, offices, a small lake and indeed hotels – a very interesting urban planning scheme. *141 rooms | Beim alten Gaswerk 3 | tel. 040 89 06 20 | www.gastwerk-hotel.de | metro bus 2, 3 Bornkampsweg*

HOTEL HAFEN HAMBURG (136 B5) (*ℳ K7*)
This hotel towers over the shipping piers, almost a symbol of the city. Rooms with views of the Elbe are considerably more expensive, but the view from the ● ☙ *Tower Bar (daily from 6pm | 12th floor)* comes without any additional cost; not only does it take tourists' breath away but even Hamburgers like to show off their city from here. *353 rooms | Seewartenstr. 9 | tel. 040 31 11 30 | www.hotel-hamburg. de | S-/U-Bahn Landungsbrücken*

HOTEL HEIMHUDE (136 C2) (*ℳ L5*)
Friendly hotel with a regular clientele. Personal service is provided in a setting

LUXURY HOTELS

Atlantic Kempinski (125 F2) (*ℳ M6*)
For almost 100 years, the Atlantic has dominated the eastern shore of the Außenalster. A portrait of Germany's last emperor, who was a guest here, hangs in the lobby. The building has recently been completely renovated and once again basks in full five-star splendour. The city's most important balls are held here. The garden terrace in the beautiful courtyard is a perfect place to be in nice weather. *254 rooms | double 290–520 euros, suites 800–5.600 euros | An der Alster 72–79 | tel. 040 2 88 80 | www.kempinski.atlantic. de | S-/U-Bahn Hauptbahnhof*

Fairmont Hotel Vier Jahreszeiten ★
(125 D3) (*ℳ L6*)
Guided for years by the steady hand of manager Ingo Peters, the Vier Jahreszeiten remains the best hotel in the city. The foyer is an oasis of tranquillity, especially beautiful at Christmas time when

it's all decorated. Anyone unsure about how to behave here can always visit the 'etiquette course' (children too!). *156 rooms | double from 310 euros, suites 510–5.000 euros | Neuer Jungfernstieg 9–14 | tel. 040 3 49 40 | www.fairmont-hvj.de | S-/U-Bahn Jungfernstieg*

Louis C. Jacob (133 E5) (*ℳ C–D6*)
Beautiful, privately owned hotel on the Elbchaussee with wonderful views of the Elbe. Lovingly designed down to the last oil painting above the fireplace. Any Blankenese local worth their salt will have got married here or at least celebrated a milestone birthday. On the ☙ terrace, immortalised by the artist Max Liebermann, you can eat divine cuisine under the lime trees. *85 rooms | double 258–315 euros, suites 385–998 euros | Elbchaussee 401–403 | tel. 040 82 25 50 | www.hotel-jacob.de | express bus 36 Sieberlingstraße*

of restrained elegance. Rooms 16–18 even have balconies. *24 rooms | Heimhuder-str. 16 | tel. 040 4 13 33 00 | www.hotel-heimhude.de | S 21, 31 Dammtor*

JUNGES HOTEL (137 E5) (*M N6*)
Great for families: children love the fold-out bunks above their parents' bed, and the whole place is really stylish, modern and congenial. The location is less attractive but it's only one stop on the U-Bahn to the Hauptbahnhof (main station). *128 rooms | Kurt-Schumacher-Allee 14 | tel. 040 41 92 30 | www.jungeshotel.de | S-/U-Bahn Berliner Tor*

LANDHAUS FLOTTBEK (133 F3) (*M E5*)
Country-house feeling in the lovely western part of Hamburg. Tastefully modernised thatched house with a delightful garden and gourmet restaurant. *25 rooms | Baron-Voght-Str. 179 | tel. 040 8 22 74 10 | www.landhaus-flottbek.de | express bus 37 Flottbeker Kirche*

LINDNER PARK HOTEL HAGENBECK
(127 E4) (*M H2*)
Animal lovers will feel right at home among the wooden crocodiles and china elephants of this zoo themed hotel. Animal noises rather than music emanate from the hall-way speakers, and a giant bronze bear welcomes guests at the entrance. A great place for the family and then of course there's Hagenbeck's Zoo just outside. *158 rooms | Hagenbeckstr. 150 | tel. 040 8 00 80 81 00 | www.lindner.de | U 2 Hagenbecks Tierpark*

NIPPON HOTEL HAMBURG
(137 E1) (*M N4*)
Japanese style of living where clear, harmonious lines predominate. Guests walk on tatami mats and the in-house Japanese restaurant has more to offer than just sushi. *42 rooms | Hofweg 75 | tel. 040 2 27*

The Atlantic Hotel is a Hamburg institution

11 40 | www.nipponhotel.de | metro bus 6 Zimmerstraße

SCANDIC ☆ ⊙ (124 B3) (*M L6*)
Typical Scandinavia: bright, chic, sustainable, as well as child friendly (including Disney Channel on TV). Wheelchair-accessible rooms. Great views from the floor to ceiling windows, also from the conference rooms – making them amongst the nicest in the city. *325 rooms | Damm-torwall 19 | tel. 040 4 32 18 70 | www.scandichotels.com | U 2 Gänsemarkt*

WEDINA (137 E4) (*M N6*)
Hamburg's literature hotel is spread across four buildings in St Georg. Writers who appear at the nearby House of Literature get to stay here for free and leave behind copies of their signed books as token of

Wood tones and warm colours: room in the Wedina Hotel

their appreciation. That sort of thing leaves an impression. *59 rooms | Gurlittstr. 23 | tel. 040 2 80 89 00 | www.hotelwedina. de/en | metro bus 6 Gurlittstraße*

YOHO (136 A2) *(ⓜ K5)*
This small designer hotel in Eimsbüttel is housed in a city mansion dating from the turn of the 20th century. The old style has been cleverly combined with the modern. It's also affordable for young people: anyone under 26 gets a discount. The Syrian restaurant *Mazza* serves superb food. *30 rooms | Moorkamp 5 | tel. 040 2 84 19 10 | www.yoho-hamburg.de | U 2 Christuskirche*

25H HAFENCITY ⭐ (141 D1) *(ⓜ M7–8)*
The rooms are called bunks, breakfast is served in the *Heimat-Hafen* (home port) restaurant and in the Club Lounge on the 1st floor people laze around on soft cushions and listen to vinyl records. And all that in the middle of brand new HafenCity. *170 rooms | Überseeallee 5 | tel. 040 2 57*

77 70 | www.25hours-hotels.com/hafen city | U 4 Überseequartier

HOTEL AM DAMMTOR (136 C3) *(ⓜ L5)*
In an old town house once occupied by students, the rooms have now been tastefully converted for paying guests. Friendly service and the campus is right outside. *33 rooms | Schlüterstr. 2 | tel. 040 4 50 05 70 | www.hotel-am-dammtor.de | S 21, 31 Dammtor*

HOTEL AM ELBUFER (134 A6) *(ⓜ E8)*
At breakfast you can look out of the window and count the containers on the enormous cargo vessels sailing past on the Elbe. The hotel is situated at the Finkenwerder quay, and from there it's just 20 minutes by Hadag ferry to the Landungsbrücken. There's hardly a more stylish way of approaching Hamburg. *15 rooms | Focksweg 40a | tel. 040 7 42 19 10 | www.hotel-am-elbufer.de*

BACKPACKERS ST PAULI (136 A4) *(ⓜ J6)*
A friendly, clean and basic place that is more suited to young people. Dorm rooms are available from about 20 euros. *10 rooms | check-in until midnight | Bernstorffstr. 98 | tel. 040 23 51 70 43 | www.backpackers-stpauli.de | metro bus 3 Bernstorffstraße*

HOTEL BAURS PARK (132 C4) *(ⓜ B6)*
Right in the middle of Blankenese, five minutes from the market square and the famous Treppenviertel with its stairs and alleys. There are also family rooms for those with children. Following the complete renovation, these are especially lovely. *24 rooms | Elbchaussee 573 | tel. 040 8 66 66 20 | www.baurspark.de | S 1, 11 Blankenese*

CRISTOBAL HOTEL (129 E6) (*M3*)
Far from the madding crowd: this small, intimate hotel is situated near the Alster in lovely Winterhude. *18 rooms | Dorotheen-str. 52 | tel. 040 3 57 03 00 | www.hotel-cristobal.de | metro bus 6, 25 Gertigstraße*

DAS FEUERSCHIFF (124 B6) (*L7*)
Bed down like an old sea dog in this red-painted former fire ship, in bunks that are small but comfortable. Listen to the Elbe lapping against the side of the wooden ship at night. INSIDER TIP Blue Monday jam sessions *(8.30pm)*, earplugs provided on the pillows. *7 rooms | City-Sporthafen Vorsetzen | tel. 040 36 25 53 | www.das-feuerschiff.de | U 3 Baumwall*

HOTEL HANSEATIN (124 B3) (*L6*)
Pretty town house opposite the Laeisz-halle, for women only. Individually styled rooms. For those travelling on their own the INSIDER TIP *Frauencafé Endlich* is the perfect place to unwind over a cup of coffee and a newspaper. *13 rooms | Dragoner-stall 11 | tel. 040 34 13 45 | www.hotel-hanseatin.de | metro bus 3 Johannes-Brahms-Platz*

KOGGE (136 A5) (*K7*)
Buildings all around get demolished or 'gentrified', but this rock 'n' roll hotel in St Pauli just keeps on going. Lots of musicians stay here and the rooms were de-signed with the help of a number of art-ists. The reception (which is also the bar) is open until 4am. *12 rooms | Bernhard-Nocht-Str. 59 | tel. 040 31 28 72 | www.kogge-hamburg.com | S 1, 3 Reeperbahn*

HOTEL MICHAELIS HOF (124 B5) (*L7*)
This hotel in the Catholic Academy offers good value for money. Whether it's be-cause of the cosy rooms or the other Christian guests, visitors automatically feel at home here. No breakfast, some rooms have use of kitchen, underground garage free of charge. *22 rooms | Herren-graben 4 | tel. 040 35 90 69 12 | www.michaelishof-hamburg.de | S 1, 3 Stadt-hausbrücke*

MOTEL HAMBURG (128 B6) (*K3*)
Most importantly: there's somewhere to park your car. And that in Eimsbüttel, right in the city centre, is worth a lot. Thanks

LOW BUDGET

▶ The view of the port from the youth hostel ☆ *Jugendherberge Auf dem Stintfang* (124 A5) (*K7*) *(357 beds | from 21.50 euros in shared rooms, older people pay 3 euros more | Alfred-Wegener-Weg 5 | tel. 040 31 34 88 | www.djh.de | S-/U-Bahn Landungsbrücken)* is unbeatable. Book well in advance!

▶ Not only for seamen: in the pleas-ant *Seemannsmission* (135 F5) (*J7*) *(38 rooms | Große Elbstr. 132 | tel. 040 30 62 20 | www.seemanns mission-altona.org | bus 111 Sandberg)* you can get a room for 45 euros (shared shower). Unrestricted views across the water.

▶ The *Schanzenstern* in the heart of the Schanzenviertel (136 A3) (*K5*) *(20 rooms | Bartelsstr. 12 | tel. 040 4 39 84 41 | www.schanzen stern.de | S-/U-Bahn Sternschanze)* was Hamburg's first low budget hotel. It could never be described as stylish and trendy, but it is welcoming and very reasonably priced (shared room from as little as 19 euros). Very popu-lar in-house ☺ organic restaurant.

Relaxed and friendly: Motel One lies between St Michael's Church and the Reeperbahn

to its pristine 1950s style the motel is now a listed building. *35 rooms | Hoheluft-chaussee 117–119 | tel. 040 4 20 41 41 | www.hamburg-hotels.de/motel | metro bus 5, 20, 25 Gärtnerstraße*

MOTEL ONE (124 A4) (*መ K7*)
The fire flickers only on screens, but that's all part of the cool, harmonious design. Despite its central location (the Reeperbahn can be seen from the upper floors) you'll get a good night's sleep as the rooms are soundproofed. The reception is open 24 hours a day; they'll even find you a dry place to park your bike. *437 rooms | Ludwig-Erhard-Straße 26 | tel. 040 35 71 89 00 | www.motel-one.com | U 3 St Pauli*

HOTEL ST ANNEN (136 A4) (*መ K6*)
Charming hotel in the peaceful part of St Pauli, with individually designed rooms and harmonious colours; garden terrace, parking out the front and internet terminals in the lobby. *32 rooms | Annenstr. 5 | tel. 040 31 77 13 0 | www.hotelstannen. de | U 3 St Pauli*

STADTHAUSHOTEL
(135 F4) (*መ J6*)
The façade may be uninviting but inside the atmosphere is all the more positive. A hostel managed by disabled people for disabled guests – and of course for others. *13 rooms | Holstenstr. 118 | tel. 040 3 89 92 00 | www.stadthaushotel.com | metro bus 15, 20, 25 Max-Brauer-Allee (Mitte)*

STELLA MARIS (124 A5) (*መ K7*)
This nice modern hotel right at the port was once home to seamen, and today you can get a simple double room for well under 100 euros. Internet terminals in the lobby. It's in the old Portuguese quarter and all around are nice little restaurants, mainly Portuguese and Spanish. *52 rooms | Reimarusstr. 12 | tel. 040 3 19 20 23 | www.stellamaris-hamburg.de | S-/U-Bahn Landungsbrücken*

SUPERBUDE ST PAULI
(136 A3) (*መ K5*)
Cool – cooler – ultra cool: this hostel is the second 'Superbude' in Hamburg, located

on the edge of the trendy Schanzenviertel, at the border with St Pauli. Incredibly creative design in an old brick block. Everyone is very friendly; triple and quad rooms also available. *84 rooms | Juliusstr. 1 | tel. 040 8 07 91 58 20 | www.superbude. de | metro bus 3 Bernstorffstraße*

HOTEL VORBACH (136 C2) (*∅ L5*)

This is where guest lecturers at the university live; occupying two nice old buildings on the Rothenbaum, the hotel is right at the campus. The place is being renovated one room at a time; the older rooms provide a more reasonably priced alternative. *116 rooms | Johnsallee 63–67 | tel. 040 44 18 20 | www.hotel-vorbach.de | U 1 Hallerstraße*

CAMPING

ELBECAMP (142 B3) (*∅ 0*)

This beach site on the banks of the Elbe at Blankenese seems almost surreal. Everything is simple but nice and indeed right on the Elbe. In summer it's quite idyllic, except for the occasional disturbance at night from barbecue parties next door. *April–Oct | tent from 5 euros, camper van from 10 euros | tel. 040 81 29 49 | www. elbecamp.de | express bus 48 Strandweg*

KNAUS-CAMP (142 C2) (*∅ 0*)

This campsite next to Ikea in Schnelsen is not at all central, but it does offer a lot in the way of comforts. Camper vans from 25.50 euros. *Wunderbrunnen 2 | tel. 040 5 59 42 25 | www.campingplatz-hamburg. de | A 7, exit Schnelsen-Nord, U 2 Niendorf Markt, then bus 191 Dornröschenweg*

B & B/FLATS

BED AND BREAKFAST

Rooms and flats in various parts of the city from 50 euros. *Office: Markusstr. 9 |*
tel. 040 4 91 56 66 | www.bed-and-break fast.de | S 1, 3 Stadthausbrücke

CLIPPER ELB-LODGE
(135 F5) (*∅ J7*)

This boarding house at the old Holzhafen has beautifully equipped apartments for temporary stays (from 150 euros per night). Locals will be really envious of the location. *57 suites | Carsten-Rehder-Str. 71 | tel. 040 80 90 10 | www.clipper-boarding houses.de | bus 111 Sandberg*

HADLEY'S BED AND BREAKFAST
(136 B2) (*∅ K4*)

Two flats in a former hospital, comfortable and centrally located. *4 rooms, 1 family room | double rooms from 85 euros | Beim Schlump 85 | tel. 040 41 78 71 | www.bed-and-breakfast-hamburg.de | metro bus 4, 15 Bundesstraße*

HENRI ★ (125 E4) (*∅ M7*)

If Don Draper of 'Mad Men' really existed he would surely live here (permanently if possible): stylish and sophisticated to the last detail, with glorious historic staircase and the beautifully designed *Henri-Bar*. You can have *abendbrod* (bread and savouries) in the open plan bar/lounge area or get a ready meal to take up to your room's own kitchenette. Double rooms 118–168 euros. *65 rooms | Bugenhagen-str. 21 | tel. 040 5 54 35 70 | www.henri-hotel.com | U 3 Mönckebergstraße*

OBERHOUSE APARTMENTS
(137 D1) (*∅ L4*)

Beautifully done out apartments: bright, friendly and nice for families, with kitchenette and fresh bread rolls delivered for breakfast. Well situated in Harvestehude, only 10 minutes' walk from the Außenalster. *32 apartments from 134 euros | Oberstr. 140 | tel. 040 41 33 39 00 | www. oberhouse.net | U 1 Klosterstern*

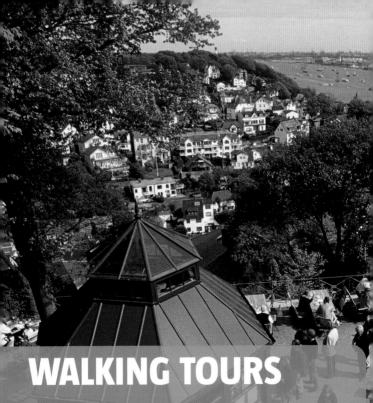

WALKING TOURS

The tours are marked in green in the street atlas, the pull-out map and on the back cover

1 UP AND DOWN THE STAIRS OF BLANKENESE

What, mountain climbing in Hamburg? But of course, in ★Blankenese! Put on your hiking boots and clamber up through the 'Positano of the North'. Duration: a good 2 hours.

The starting point is Blankenese station. An initial warm-up is provided by the short climb to the Gossler-Haus, located to the right above the Blankeneser Landstraße. For decades, the splendid white building was used as a local government office, like so many beautiful old mansions in the west of Hamburg; today it is the conference centre of a private university. Then it's back down and across the lights, where the first refreshments await: scones in Lühmanns Café *(daily | Blankeneser Landstr. 29 | tel. 040 86 34 42)*. Continue along Kirschtenstraße, with the old grammar school on the left, over the zebra crossing and across the car park to reach the Hessepark. Pass the Hessehaus, now a school, on the right, and then exit the park on the right.

You come out at the Charitas Bischoff steps, where the descent begins, in the heart of the Treppenviertel. To the left and right the walls of the old houses are almost at your fingertips, separated only by steep steps and narrow paths. You can see into

Photo: Blankenese from the Süllberg

Blankenese, HafenCity, Außenalster and Wilhelmsburg: Hamburg is a great place for walkers, cyclists and paddlers

the gardens and through kitchen windows. Above and to the right are the flags atop the Süllberg, while below shines the River Elbe. It is easy to understand why everyone wants to come and live here, but that is difficult because many of the old captains' houses have been in the same family for generations.

The route continues downhill, and you cross the Blankeneser Hauptstraße (high

street). Perhaps the 'mountain goat' mini-bus is just passing, in which case you can take a ride along the banks of the Elbe. It's nicer though to continue downhill via the Schlagemihls steps. Meeting the serpentine high street once again, cross over it and, just past house number 38, turn left into Hans-Lange-Straße (this is just one route you can take). You're now almost at the Elbe. Thinking of a stroll on the warm sand, or a fish roll at the jetty? Or maybe even a coffee at the INSIDER TIP ► Elbkrämer? The small shop with its bistro *(open only at weekends)* is right in front of you. But of course you want to climb again: just where the last cars are parked, go right up the Elbterrasse for a short distance. Notice the historic **Dreehuhs** houses built for three fishermen's families (numbers 4–6) and then take the Süllberg-Treppe (steps) up to the right. Watch out, it gets very steep here. At the top go left along the Süllberg-terrasse for a few feet to arrive at the **Kaffeegarten Schuldt** *(Tue–Sun 2pm–9pm, Nov–April Sat/Sun 1pm–6pm | tel. 040 86 24 11)*, which has been in the same family for 130 years. The cake is home-baked, the atmosphere unique. Now you've almost made it. Go left out of the café and follow the Süllbergterrasse round for about 200m, before taking the next path up to the left. After a few steps you'll arrive at the final ascent to the ✹ **Süllberg**, a luxury restaurant → p. 64, hotel and beer garden. A beautiful view over the Elbe with a cool glass of *Weißbier*: what bliss!

CYCLE TOUR THROUGH HAFENCITY

The tour is only about 3.5km/ 2mi long, but you should allow at least 2 hours. It will take you right through HafenCity, across bridges, past building sites, and includes detours into the Speicherstadt. Discover a district in which changes are happening almost every week, between gleaming office blocks and life at street level that's just starting to get going. There are lots of cafés on the route so it's probably enough just to take a water bottle.

The starting point is the Stadtrad (city bike) depot at the Strandkai in front of the **Unileverhaus** → p. 47. Here is the playground that city kids have already made their own. You can rent out two bikes on one ticket → p. 112. Diagonally opposite lies the cruise ship terminal. If you're there during the season, you might see a luxury liner such as the 'Aida' at anchor. Pass the terminal on your right and cycle around the left-hand bend past the new U4 station

Brave new world: 'Der Spiegel' headquarters and the Deichtorcenter

to the heating plant and San-Francisco-Straße. Turn left into the Überseequartier (overseas quarter): there are some chic shops and cafés, but it's mostly still a barren emptiness. Keep to the right and cross the Osakaallee. Just before the Busanbrücke at the Magdeburger Hafen you will see the Störtebeker Memorial → p. 47, and right opposite the magnificent warehouse building of the Maritime Museum → p. 45. Building work is still going on here, including the new Greenpeace headquarters. Battle your way through as far as Shanghaiallee, where they are building the first blocks of social housing in HafenCity as well as the future green lung of the new district, Lohsepark. The balloon that you might see floating somewhere to the northeast is the Highflyer → p. 14, which you can always stop and watch for a while. Cycle left along the Shanghaiallee and stop for some refreshment in the small chapel of the Ecumenical Forum → p. 46. The Weltcafé Elbfaire serves fair trade coffee. Diagonally opposite is the Prototyp Automobile Museum → p. 46. Turn right there: there's a lot of building going on here too and the street layout is constantly changing. You will reach Lohseplatz, once the location of the Hanover railway station. It was from here between 1940 and 1945 that deportation transports left Hamburg for the Nazi death camps. A simple plaque commemorates the events. Continue cycling; opposite, on the other side of the canal, you can see straight across to the magnificent new headquarters of Germany's famous news magazine, 'Der Spiegel'. Newspaper crisis? Not at 'Der Spiegel' apparently. Continue along the Steinschanze as far as the railway bridge. There, right under the tracks, is an odd, lopsided brick house. It is the listed building the Oberhafen-Kantine → p. 70, once a snack bar for dockworkers. Suitably fortified you can cross the lower deck of the

bridge to the other side, circle round the bridge supports and voilà: you've arrived at the Deichtorhallen → p. 43 almost in the centre of the city. Cross the square and the wide street at the pedestrian crossing. The building that you pass on the left is the Deichtorcenter, whose 10-storey prism shaped façade is a throwback to the Chilehaus. At the crossing turn left along the Dovenfleet canal which runs parallel to the Speicherstadt. After about 300m you'll pass the beautiful Katharinenkirche (Church of St Catherine). Now push your bike across the street and on to the flood protection barrier (cycling is forbidden here). The Zollkanal is spanned by the double-decker Kibbelstegbrücke, which also serves as an emergency exit for HafenCity; emergency vehicles use this route. Pedestrians walk above and cyclists take the ramp down to the lower deck and across into the Speicherstadt → p. 42. It's worth taking a detour into Pickhuben Street: at the very first entrance you can look into the courtyard and marvel at the oriel windows and brickwork patterning. The second part of the bridge leads across the Brooksfleet and through to Große Grasbrook, where after 100m you will arrive at the Magellan Terraces with the Elbphilharmonie pavilion and the traditional port. At the moment this is the liveliest place in HafenCity when the weather's nice. Return your bikes back to the Unilever building now just 200m away, and take a peaceful stroll along the waterfront.

3 ONCE AROUND THE AUSSENALSTER

The nice path around the ★ Außenalster will show you many sides of Hamburg: sport and culture, civic pride and patronage. Duration: 2–3 hours.

A lovely part of Hamburg: boats on the Außenalster

The route around the Außenalster is 7.5km/ 4.5mi long. It is ideal for jogging, and this is exactly what countless Hamburgers do every day. But you have better to do. A nice place to start your tour is the radiant white **Hotel Atlantic** (An der Alster 72–79 → p. 94), which dates back to 1909. At that time the cruise industry was experiencing its first boom, and it was in the Atlantic that the wealthy passengers waited to board their ships. Today in the lobby you might bump into Germany's rock legend Udo Lindenberg, who has lived here for years. Cross the road to the Alster shore and turn to the right. Perhaps you'd like to obtain a sailing licence? You can do that at the ● **Pieper Sailing School** (Atlanticsteg | tel. 040 24 75 78 | www. segelschule-pieper.de). Note: the Alster has its own rules: boats on the right (starboard) always have priority, as of course do the Alster steamers. At Schwanenwik 38 is the **Literaturhaus** (daily | tel. 040 22 70 20 11 | www.literaturhaus-hamburg.de), a place where you could spend a whole day, with wonderful stucco decorated ballroom (now the Literaturhauscafé), bookstore and many readings. A little further along the shore the trendy **Alsterperle** (daily) is a good place to take a short break. Housed in a converted public toilet, the snack bar is tiny, but has cult status because it's such a wonderful place to relax over a beer and to enjoy the great views over the Alster – preferably at sunset.

The walk continues along the ☼ **Schöne Aussicht**. The name says it all as it means 'beautiful view' in German, and indeed the view back to the city gets progressively more beautiful here. Don't panic if see a lot of policemen in front of house number 26. They'll be there for security reasons. Built by Martin Haller in 1868, this Alster villa is the official **guest house of the Senate**, the city parliament. The Queen and the Duke of Edinburgh stayed here on their official visit to the city in 1965, later to be followed by Charles and Diana. A little further on stands a completely different kind of building: the **Imam Ali Mosque**. Built in 1961, today it is an important centre for Hamburg's Shia

Muslim community. Right opposite we have a return to good old Hanseatic values: the NRV is Hamburg's most traditional sailing club, where you can only join if you have two sponsors. You can't get lost at this point, even though the road now veers briefly away from the Alster; after a short stretch along Sierichstrasse you turn back left along Bellevue with its row of magnificent villas overlooking the lake.

At the top end of the Alster, at the Krugkoppelbrücke, you could think about taking a break, perhaps on the lovely terrace of the Bobby Reich Restaurant → p. 67. If it's now too far for you to walk back, you can always take one of the Alster steamers and cruise back to the Jungfernstieg in comfort. Otherwise continue walking along the green banks of the western shore. The ● Alsterpark has only been accessible to the public since 1953. Previously the land belonged to the private villas along Harvestehuder Weg. It gets packed here on sunny weekends, when it's difficult to find a free seat on one of those nice wooden benches that dot the park. House number 42 is still the residence of the family firm Hoffmann and Campe, the German poet Heinrich Heine's publisher. You next pass Pöseldorf where the designer Jil Sander began her career on Milchstrasse. Today, there are several fine galleries and a few chic shops, cafés and restaurants there. Milchstraße 12, the former Budge Palais, is now home to the city's music academy. At the end of the walk is another 'White House': the US Consulate. In Nazi times it housed the offices of the Hamburg Gauleiter, Karl Kaufmann. Since 2001 the street in front has been completely closed off (take the path to the left along the water's edge, with its romantically positioned benches). If you still haven't had enough: the hiking path INSIDER TIP ▶ Alsterwanderweg leads from here along the Elbe through to the city centre. Take the pedestrian tunnel under the Kennedy and Lombard bridges and at the Jungfernstieg turn into the Alster arcades, then go straight along the Alsterfleet to the Schaartorschleuse. The Alster, fine villas, the city, the canals and now the Elbe: this is about as varied as a stroll as can be.

THROUGH WILHELMSBURG BY CANOE

Awaken your pioneering spirit and paddle a canoe through Wilhelmsburg. The district is the largest inhabited river island in Europe and in 2013 was the setting of the International Garden Show. Reason enough to discover the burgeoning area from the water. Children can join the tour without difficulty.

The starting point is the Zum Anleger beer garden on the Ernst August Kanal, which provides canoe rentals *(Mon–Sat from 11.30am, Sun from 10am, season May–3 Oct, limited times in winter | Vogelhüttendeich 123 | tel. 040 86 68 77 81 | www.zum-anleger.de)*. It is easy to reach on foot or by number 13 bus from Veddel S-Bahn station. There's a discount if you hire canoes for more than 3 hours, and that's about the time it takes for the approx. 8km/5mi tour towards Wilhelmsburger Dove-Elbe. You'll be amazed: the canal and Elbe tributary were once an excursion destination for Hamburgers; today orchids blossom along the enchanted banks. You can also paddle along the smaller canals and take a detour to the Assmannkanal, which was dug for the International Garden Show (IGS) and can now be used as a circuit by canoeing enthusiasts. The ultimate aim is to be able to cross the whole of Wilhelmsburg using the waterways. And if you dare to cross the Elbe you can even paddle all the way from the Hamburg to the Wilhelmsburg town hall.

TRAVEL WITH KIDS

There are big ships in the harbour and little paddleboats on the Alster, sand for building castles along the Elbe and many museums that have children's programmes and even a hotel for children. What more could a family want?

HAGENBECKS TIERPARK ★ ●
(127 E4) (⌂ H2)

This is one of the most beautiful landscaped zoos in the world, run for generations by the Hagenbeck family. In the exciting tropical aquarium look out for the INSIDER TIP glowing blue scorpions, quite amazing! Other highlights include a sensational orang-utan house, a new arctic area and elephants which can be hand fed. There are also lions, tigers, bears, bison, porcupines, mountain goats, lamas and meerkats, etc., not to mention the nice playgrounds and the *Jungle Nights* in the summer. *March–June, Sept/Oct daily 9am–6pm, July/Aug 9am–7pm, Nov–Feb 9am–4.30pm | combined ticket for park and aquarium (also available individually) 30 euros, children 21 euros | Lokstedter Grenzstr. 2 | tel. 040 5 30 03 30 | www.hagenbeck.de | U 2 Hagenbecks Tierpark*

KINDERHOTEL BENGEL UND ENGEL
(127 F6) (⌂ J3–4)

A children's hotel just like those for adults: reception desk, welcome cocktail, towels and attentive carers. There are 8 places for children aged between one and 12. Childcare from 6pm to 9am the following day, 59 euros incl. meals. *Stellinger Weg 49 | tel. 040 43 17 94 90 | www.bengel-engel.de | U 2 Lutterothstraße*

MUSEUMS

All state museums are INSIDER TIP free of charge for children under 18. And all museums, including the private ones, offer special children's programmes. Just ask at the *Museum Information Service (tel. 040 4 28 13 10 | www.museumsdienst.hamburg.de)*. Fun for children, as well as being inexpensive, is the customs museum *Zollmuseum (125 D5) (⌂ M7) (Tue–Sun 10am–5pm | admission 2 euros | Alter Wandrahm 16 | www.museum.zoll.de | U 1 Meßberg)* in the Speicherstadt warehouse district. The University's zoological collection with its array of stuffed animals, ● *Zoologische Sammlung (136 B2) (⌂ L5) (Tue–Sun 10am–5pm | Martin-Luther-King-*

The perfect city for families: Hamburg is ideal for a short outing with the children: animals, boats, museums and the theatre

Platz 3 | www.biologie.uni-hamburg.de | metro bus 4, 5 Grindelhof) is free of charge. Here you can also see INSIDER TIP a walrus named Antje, familiar to many Germans from TV.

SHOPPING WITH CHILDREN

At *Stilwerk* (135 F5) (*111 J7*) you don't just get chic designer shops but also a free child-minding service on Sat *(from age 4 | Große Elbstr. 68 | tel. 040 30 62 11 00 | www.stilwerk.de)*. At Christmas time there are steamers moored at the Jungfernstieg jetty (125 D3) (*111 M6*) where children can listen to fairytales or bake biscuits while their parents shop for Christmas presents.

CHILDREN'S THEATRE/ALLEETHEATER
(135 E4) (*111 H6*)

This is where children are taken seriously – as has been the case since 1968. In the evening there are operas for grown-ups.

Tickets from 14 euros, performances usually on Fri, Sat and Sun. *Max-Brauer-Allee 76 | tel. 040 38 25 38 | www.theater-fuer-kinder.de | metro bus 15, 20, 25 Gerichts-straße*

WILLKOMMHÖFT/WELCOME POINT
(142 B3) (*111 O*)

At the Wedel welcome point ships sailing into or out of Hamburg are greeted or wished 'bon voyage' with music and their national anthem. Retired captains conduct a flag ceremony and record the ship's tonnage, length and land of origin. On the huge terrace and at the stalls in front you can get anything you like to eat and drink. And afterwards you can take a little walk along the Elbe. A great excursion for the whole family! *Wedel | Schulauer Fährhaus | daily from 9am | admission 3 euros | www.schulauer-faehrhaus.de | S 1 Wedel, then bus 189 Elbstraße*

FESTIVALS & EVENTS

The Hanseatics love their festivals: the 'Dom' fair on the Heiligengeistfeld (held three times a year), the show jumping and derby in Klein Flottbek as well as the many neighbourhood festivals such as the *Altonale* in Ottensen or similar events in St Georg, Eimsbüttel and Winterhude (dates: *english.hamburg.de*).

PUBLIC HOLIDAYS

1 Jan; Good Friday; Easter Monday; 1 May; Ascension Day; Whit Monday; 3 Oct *(German Unity Day)*; 25/26 Dec

FESTIVALS

APRIL/MAY

▶ *Marathon:* for amateurs and professionals. *www.marathon-hamburg.de;* ▶ *Lange Nacht der Museen:* the museums are open late into the night, free shuttle buses. *www.langenachtdermuseen.hamburg.de;* ▶ ★ *Hafengeburtstag (beginning of May):* a huge party is held along the shipping piers to celebrate the port anniversary – tall ships' parade and the 'tug dance'. *www.hafengeburtstag.de;*

▶ *Elbjazz Festival:* still young and crazy, jazz at its best in and around the port. *www.elbjazz.de*

MAY/JUNE

▶ *Japanese Cherry Blossom Festival:* beautiful fireworks display around the Alster; ▶ *German Show Jumping and Dressage Derby in Klein Flottbek:* one of the most famous meets in the world. *engarde.de*

JUNE/JULY

▶ *Jungle Nights at Hagenbeck:* a zoo is turned into a jungle, on several Saturdays. *tel. 040 5 30 03 30;* ▶ *Altonale:* art and culture at the district fair in0 Altona. *www.altonale.de;* ▶ *Hamburg Jazz Open:* open-air Jazz in Planten un Blomen. *End of June, www.jazzbuero-hamburg.de;* ▶ *Derby week:* fast horses and gorgeous hats at Hamburg Horn. *Rennbahnstraße 96;* ▶ *Hamburg Ballet Days:* John Neumeier's ballet never fails to excite. *www.hamburg-ballett.de;* ▶ *Schlagermove:* the music floats of the 'hit parade', which pays homage to the 1970s, go right through St Pauli, accompanied by thousands of fans in fancy dress. *www.schlagermove.de*

Whether sport, the anniversary of the port or a street party – the Hamburgers always like an excuse to celebrate

JULY/AUGUST

▶ **INSIDER TIP** *Hamburg 'Jedermann':* spectacular open-air theatre does 'Everyman' in the Speicherstadt; on seven weekends. *www.hamburger-jedermann.de;*
▶ *Triathlon:* swimming, cycling and running in the city. *www.hamburg-triathlon.org;* ▶ *Vattenfall Cyclassics:* cycle race for professionals and amateurs alike, out into the suburbs. *www.vattenfall-cyclassics.de*
▶ *Christopher Street Day:* originally just for the gay and lesbian community, today this is a colourful street festival for all, complete with parade.*www.csd-hamburg.com;*
▶ *Dockville Festival:* three-day music and art spectacle in Wilhelmsburg. *www.dockville.de;* ▶ *Alstervergnügen:* stalls with food and drink, music and amateur dramatics all around the Binnenalster lake

SEPTEMBER/OCTOBER

▶ *Harbour Front Literaturfestival:* literature festival that takes place primarily in HafenCity as well as other reading locations on the Elbe. *www.harbourfront-hamburg.com;*
▶ *Night of the Churches:* more than 100 churches open their doors between 6pm and midnight and offer services, music, art and literature. And: the Hamburgers come in droves. *www.ndkh.de;* ▶ *Reeperbahnfestival:* it really rocks in the neighbourhood's music clubs. *End Sept, www.reeperbahnfestival.com;* ▶ *Hamburg International Film Festival:* a must for film buffs. *www.filmfesthamburg.de*

NOVEMBER/DECEMBER

▶ *Markt der Völker:* Christmas market in the Ethnology Museum, with presents from around the world; ▶ *Weihnachtsmarkt:* Christmas market on the town hall square, the Rathausmarkt
▶ *Silvesterfeuerwerk:* New Year's firework display at the port.

LINKS, BLOGS, APPS & MORE

LINKS

▶ english.hamburg.de Hamburg's official tourism website, providing information on accommodation, culture, shopping, public transport, car rental, restaurants, music and sports events, museums and other attractions, and living in Hamburg. Includes videos

▶ www.germany.travel/en German tourism website ideal site for those wanting to explore the country further

▶ eventful.com/hamburg/events comprehensive coverage of what's going on in the city and upcoming concerts and gigs

▶ www.hafencity.com/en for the latest news on HafenCity, plus upcoming events

▶ www.hvv.de/en all the information you need about public transport in Hamburg, plus bookings and tickets

▶ www.hempels-musictour.com/en Stefanie Hempel is the originator of the musical Beatles-Tour in Hamburg. Follow her and her ukelele in the tracks of the Fab Four across the famous red light district of St Pauli

BLOGS & FORUMS

▶ www.expat-blog.com/en/directory/europe/germany/hamburg there is a contingent of expatriate Brits, Americans and others in Hamburg. Pictures, classified ads and a very lively forum. If you need specific information, then best to ask someone who lives there

▶ www.toytowngermany.com is the best online forum for expats in Germany and the topics of discussion include local news, reviews, relocation issues as well as legal and financial advice. The forum also organises a number of live social events

▶ www.internations.org/hamburg-expats a great forum for people intending to stay longer in the city, or those just getting established

Regardless of whether you are still preparing your trip or already in Hamburg: these addresses will provide you with more information, videos and networks to make your holiday even more enjoyable

▶ www.spottedbylocals.com/hamburg some really useful tips and suggestions from locals across a broad range of themes of interest to the visitor, from restaurants to music venues and relaxation to shopping

▶ www.360cities.net the 360° panoramic photos give an all-round view of top sights. Check out the rotating views of the Speicherstadt by night, the view from the tower of St Michael's Church, the town hall square and many other attractions

VIDEOS & PODCASTS

▶ www.youtube.com search for any topic you like such as 'Fischmarkt', 'HafenCity' or 'Reeperbahn' to get revealing insights into the real Hamburg

▶ www.miniatur-wunderland.de the best videos from Miniatur-Wunderland, Hamburg's most visited attraction.

▶ Hamburg at a Glance: Sights, Tips & Tours produced by the Hamburg Tourist Board. Hamburg's most exciting sights at a glance

▶ TripAdvisor all the usual TripAdvisor information and booking facilities for your tablet or mobile

▶ Hamburg Map & Walks this handy app has detailed tour routes is ideal to use to explore the city at your own pace and aims to make you feel as though you are being taken around by a local guide.

APPS

▶ www.couchsurfing.org describes itself as the largest traveller community. You don't have to sign up to find profiles of travellers or locals. Click 'Browse People' and then enter 'Hamburg' in the search field

▶ www.travelpod.com/s/hamburg?st=user for some first-hand reports, travel blogs, photos and a wide selection of videos by other international Hamburg tourists

▶ www.airbnb.com the popular site for travellers who prefer to stay in private accommodation offered by locals.

NETWORK

TRAVEL TIPS

ARRIVAL

Along the north-south axis via the A7 motorway (Flensburg-Hanover/ Kassel); from the east and west via the A1 (Lübeck/Bremen); from Berlin via the A24 and from Heide/Husum via the A23. There are often traffic jams on the A7 around the Elbe Tunnel during rush hour. For information on public parking see: *english. hamburg.de/1-arrival-in-hamburg-np*

Hamburg has four intercity stations: Hauptbahnhof (with connections to all underground and suburban), Dammtor (CCH), Altona and Harburg. ICEs link Hamburg with all major German cities. *www. bahn.de/i/view/GBR/en/index.shtml*

Hamburg International Airport is centrally located in the north of the city (Fuhlsbüttel). Airport Office: *tel. 040 5 07 50 | www.hamburg-airport.de*. From there you can easily reach the centre by public transport: the S1 leaves Hamburg-Airport every 10 minutes and it takes just 25 minutes to Hauptbahnhof. There are four bus services and a night bus that leave the Airport Plaza for various U-Bahn stations. Depending on the destination a taxi into the city takes between 20 and 40 minutes and costs from 26 euros. The airport transfer service links Hamburg with northern Germany and the Bremen area.

BANKS

Normal opening hours are 10am–5pm on weekdays; some banks however are open until 2pm on Saturdays. Cash dispensers *(Geldautomat)* can be found everywhere.

BOAT/WALKING TOURS

Stattreisen Hamburg e. V. (tel. 040 87 08 01 00 | www.stattreisen-hamburg.de) offers a number of different tours of the city including some unusual topics like the 'Harbour for Children' as well as boat tours. *StadtkulTour (tel. 040 36 62 69 | www. hamburger-nachtwaechter.de):* tours following in the footsteps of Heinrich Heine or torchlight tours around the warehouse district of Speicherstadt. *March–Oct Sat 8.30pm | U-Bahnhof Baumwall | 15 euros including torches.*
Rock 'n' Roll live (March–Oct Sat 6pm | 2.5hrs | 25 euros | from U-Bahn Feldstraße | tel. 040 30 03 37 90 | www.hempels-music tour.de/en/): on her Beatles Tour through St Pauli the musician Stefanie Hempel relates some amazing stories about the Fab Four, the clubs and the Reeperbahn during the 1960s, and does brilliant renditions of Beatles numbers on her ukulele (in winter as a bus tour).

RESPONSIBLE TRAVEL

It doesn't take a lot to be environmentally friendly whilst travelling. Don't just think about your carbon footprint whilst flying to and from your holiday destination but also about how you can protect nature and culture abroad. As a tourist it is especially important to respect nature, look out for local products, cycle instead of driving, save water and much more. If you would like to find out more about eco-tourism please visit: *www.ecotourism.org*

From arrival to weather

Holiday from start to finish: the most important addresses and information for your Hamburg trip

CYCLING

There are many cycle paths, which make trips with the children that much easier. Bicycles can be taken on the HVV free of charge – at any time of the day during school summer holidays, otherwise not before 9am or between 4–6pm, Mon–Fri. The bright red ● INSIDER TIP Hamburg City Bikes are a good way of getting from A to B. There are 72 rental points and around 1,000 bikes, with more to come. This is how it works: the initial payment of 5 euros includes a travel 'credit'; the first 30 minutes are free of charge and each minute after that is charged at 8 cents. Payment can be made at each terminal with an EC card, a credit/debit card or by phone. Further information: www.stadtradhamburg.de or tel. 040 8 22 18 81 00.

Hamburg-Radtour is one of several companies offering guided tours by bike (meeting point Dammtor | tel. 040 81 99 22 39 | www.hamburg-radtour.de).

City bikes and ladies cycles can be rented cheaply from the Fahrradstation at the university (from 12 euros/day) (Schlüterstraße 11 | tel. 040 8 22 18 81 00 | www.fahrradstation-hh.de).

EMERGENCIES

Police: tel. 110; fire brigade/ambulance: tel. 112; medical emergency: tel. 040 22 80 22 (24-hr service); emergency doctor's surgery: Stresemannstr. 54 (136 A3) (ⓜ G5) | Mon/Tue, Thu/Fri 7pm–midnight, Wed 1pm–midnight, Sat/Sun 7am–midnight; emergency dental service: tel. 01805 05 05 18 (*); duty chemist: tel. 0800 0 02 28 33

INFORMATION

HAMBURG TOURISM
Postfach 102 249 | 20 015 Hamburg |

CURRENCY CONVERTER

£	€	€	£
1	1.20	1	0.85
3	3.60	3	2.55
5	6	5	4.25
13	15.60	13	11
40	48	40	34
75	90	75	64
120	144	120	100
250	300	250	210
500	600	500	425

$	€	€	$
1	0.75	1	1.30
3	2.30	3	3.90
5	3.80	5	6.50
13	10	13	17
40	30	40	50
75	55	75	97
120	90	120	155
250	185	250	325
500	370	500	650

For current exchange rates see www.xe.com

tel. +49 (0)40 30 05 13 00 | Mon–Sat 9am–7pm | www.hamburg-travel.com

TOURIST INFORMATION
– Railway Station (exit Kirchenallee) | Mon–Sat 9am–7pm, Sun 10am–6pm
– Landungsbrücken (between piers 4 and 5) | Sun–Wed 9am–6pm, Thu–Sat 9am–7pm

INTERNET

In the city centre laptops work almost anywhere and many cafés and restaurants often display signs offering 'free WLAN' on the door.

BUDGETING

Cappuccino	£2.30/$3.60
	at a café
Musical	£60–80/$100–130
	medium price category
Wine	from £3.30/$5.20
	per glass at a bar
Pizza	from £6.50/$10.50
	at a restaurant
Boat trip	approx. £11.50/$18
	for a harbour round trip
Bus ride	£1.50/$2.50
	for a single journey

Informative: *www.hamburg-travel.com, english.hamburg.de;* for programme of events see local daily newspapers and city magazines (in German): *www.mopo.de, www.abendblatt.de, www.szene-hamburg. de;* the online city map is useful: *www. hamburg.de/stadtplan;* timetable information: *www.hvv.de*

PUBLIC TRANSPORT

Hamburg has a well-developed public transport system, operated by the HVV (Hamburg Transport Authority). Single, day and group tickets (also valid for the Hadag Elbe ferries) are available from vending machines; children under 6 years of age travel free. At weekends and on public holidays, the most important bus routes and the S- and U-Bahn lines within the Hamburg city area run around the clock. In addition to covering public transport, the *Hamburg Card* (available for 1, 3 or 5 days) allows discounts on admission fees to museums, on theatre tickets, in certain restaurants and on sightseeing tours of the city, port and Alster: day passes (1 adult/3 children) 8.90 euros, group tickets (up to 5 people) 14.90 euros, three-day ticket 21.90 euros (groups 38.90 euros). For those who want to explore the surrounding area as well, the *Hamburg Card plus Region* is recommended. The ticket is valid in the whole of the wider HVV area, e.g. to Stade or Bad Segeberg, and includes more than 130 reductions at tourist sights and in shops (day pass for 1 adult/3 children under 15 19.90 euros; groups up to 5 people 28.50 euros; 3-day pass 49.90 euros/79.90 euros). Available from all HVV service points, the Tourist Information Office, and online at *www.hamburg-travel.com.* For HVV timetable information: *tel. 040 194 49,* though it works quicker by text: simply enter *Start!Ziel!* and send to the number *5 53 55.* Further information: *www.hvv.de/en/index.php*

SIGHTSEEING TOURS

For those new to the city, the red double-decker hop-on hop-off buses and *Hummelbahn* are to be recommended *(summer 9.30am–5pm every 30min; winter hourly 10am–4pm, Sat/Sun every 30min | 17.50 euros | tel. 040 7 92 89 79 | www.die-roten-doppeldecker.de/en.html).* The tours start from the main railway station (Hauptbahnhof), exit Kirchenallee, and from the Landungsbrücken piers. The day pass allows passengers to hop on and off at any stop. Hamburg-Rundfahrt (blue buses): *tel. 040 6 41 37 31 | www.hansa-rundfahrt.de*

You can see the port and its ships on the 3-hour ● INSIDER TIP 'Trip of the Giants' (Gigantentour) laid on by *Jasperreisen (Sat/Sun, April–Oct also Wed, Fri | departs Vorsetzen/Überseebrücke | 30 euros, children 15 euros | booking and passport/ID card essential | tel. 040 22 71 06 10 | www. jasper.de).*

Bicycle-rickshaws: young cyclists will pedal you around the city. *April–Oct | from 5 euros | tel. 0162 108 90 20 | www.trimotion. de; tel. 0177 7 36 70 42 | www.pedalotours. de*

SWIMMING

The renovated ● INSIDER TIP *Holthusenbad (Goernestr. 21 | U 1, 3 Kellinghusenstraße)* in Eppendorf has a variety of bathing options, including wave pool, heated outdoor pool and sauna. Close to the centre in St Georg is the *Alsterschwimmhalle (Ifflandstr. 21 | U 1, 3 Lübecker Straße)* with its 50m/165ft pool. In summer the *natural pool Naturbad Stadtparksee (Südring 5b | U 3 Saarlandstraße)* is pure bliss. For all pools: *tel. 040 18 88 90 | www. baederland.de*

TAXI

Autoruf Taxi: *tel. 040 44 10 11*; Das Taxi: *tel. 040 22 11 22*; Hansa Funktaxi: *tel. 040 211211*; Taxi Hamburg: *tel. 040 66 66 66*

THEATRE & CONCERT TICKETS

– Konzertkasse Gerdes *(Rothenbaumchaussee 77 | tel. 040 45 03 50 60)*
– Konzertkasse Hauptbahnhof *(in the Tourist Information Office | tel. 040 32 87 38 54)*
– Konzertkasse Mercado Altona *(in the Hugendubel book shop | Ottenser Hauptstr. 10 | tel. 040 39 88 49 10)*
– Konzertkasse Schanze *(Schanzenstr. 5 | tel. 040 38 65 51 95)*

WEATHER IN HAMBURG

	Jan	Feb	March	April	May	June	July	Aug	Sept	Oct	Nov	Dec
Daytime temperatures in °C/°F	2/36	3/37	8/46	13/55	18/64	22/72	23/73	23/73	19/66	13/55	7/45	4/39
Nighttime temperatures in °C/°F	–3/27	–3/27	0/32	3/37	7/45	11/52	13/55	13/15	10/50	6/43	2/36	–1/30
Sunshine hours/day	2	2	4	6	8	8	7	6	6	4	2	1
Water temperatures in °C/°F	12/54	10/50	8/46	10/50	10/50	10/50	12/54	11/52	10/50	10/50	11/52	11/52

USEFUL PHRASES GERMAN

PRONUNCIATION

We have provided a simple pronunciation aid for the german words
(see the square brackets). Note the following:

ch	usually like ch in Scottish "loch", shown here as [kh]
g	hard as in "get"
ß	is a double s
ä	like the vowel in "fair" or "bear"
ö	a little like er as in "her"
ü	is spoken as ee with rounded lips, like the French "tu"
ie	is ee as in "fee", but ei is like "height", shown here as [ei]
'	stress on the following syllable

IN BRIEF

Yes/No/Maybe	Ja [yah]/Nein [nein]/Vielleicht [fee'leikht]
Please/Thank you	Bitte ['bi-te]/Danke ['dan-ke]
Sorry	Entschuldige [ent'shul-di-ge]
Excuse me, please	Entschuldigen Sie [ent'shul-di-gen zee]
May I ...?/ Pardon?	Darf ich ...? [darf ikh]/Wie bitte? [vee 'bi-te]
I would like to .../	Ich möchte ... [ikh 'merkh-te]/
have you got ...?	Haben Sie ...? ['hab-en zee]
How much is ...?	Wie viel kostet ...? [vee-feel 'koss-tet]
I (don't) like this	Das gefällt mir/nicht [das ge-'felt meer/nikht]
good/bad	gut/schlecht [goot/shlekht]
broken/doesn't work	kaputt [ka-'put]/funktioniert nicht/ funk-tsion-'eert nikht]
too much/much/little	(zu) viel/wenig [tsoo feel/'vay-nikh]
Help!/Attention!/ Caution!	Hilfe! ['hil-fe]/Achtung! [akh-'tung]/ Vorsicht! ['for-sikht]
ambulance	Krankenwagen ['kran-ken-vaa-gen]/ Notarzt ['note-aatst]
police/fire brigade	Polizei [pol-i-'tsei]/Feuerwehr ['foy-er-vayr]
danger/dangerous	Gefahr [ge-'far]/gefährlich [ge-'fair-likh]

GREETINGS, FAREWELL

Good morning!/after-noon!/evening!/night!	Gute(n) Morgen ['goo-ten 'mor-gen]/Tag [taag]/ Abend ['aa-bent]/Nacht [nakht]
Hello!/goodbye!	Hallo ['ha-llo]/Auf Wiedersehen [owf 'vee-der-zayn]

Sprichst du Deutsch?

"Do you speak German?" This guide will help you to say the basic words and phrases in German

See you!	Tschüss [chüss]
My name is ...	Ich heiße ... [ikh 'hei-sse]
What's your name?	Wie heißt Du [vee heist doo]/ heißen Sie? ['heiss-en zee]
I'm from ...	Ich komme aus ... [ikh 'ko-mme ows]

DATE & TIME

Monday/Tuesday	Montag ['moan-tag]/Dienstag ['deens-tag]
Wednesday/Thursday	Mittwoch ['mit-vokh]/Donnerstag ['don-ers-tag]
Friday/Saturday	Freitag ['frei-tag]/Samstag ['zams-tag]
Sunday/holiday	Sonntag ['zon-tag]/Feiertag ['fire-tag]
today/tomorrow/ yesterday	heute ['hoy-te]/morgen ['mor-gen]/ gestern ['gess-tern]
hour/minute	Stunde ['shtun-de]/Minute [min-'oo-te]
day/night/week	Tag [tag]/Nacht [nakht]/Woche ['vo-khe]
What time is it?	Wie viel Uhr ist es? ['vee-feel oor ist es]
It's three o'clock	Es ist drei Uhr [ez ist drei oor]

TRAVEL

open/closed	offen ['off-en]/geschlossen [ge-'shloss-en]
entrance (vehicles)	Zufahrt ['tsoo-faat]
entrance/exit	Eingang ['ein-gang]/Ausgang ['ows-gang]
arrival/departure (flight)	Ankunft ['an-kunft]/Abflug ['ap-floog]
toilets/restrooms / ladies/gentlemen	Toiletten [twa-'let-en]/ Damen ['daa-men]/Herren ['her-en]
(no) drinking water	(kein) Trinkwasser [(kein) 'trink-vass-er]
Where is ...?/Where are ...?	Wo ist ...? [vo ist]/Wo sind ...? [vo zint]
left/right	links [links]/rechts [rekhts]
straight ahead/back	geradeaus [ge-raa-de-'ows]/zurück [tsoo-'rük]
close/far	nah [naa]/weit [veit]
taxi/cab	Taxi ['tak-si]
bus stop/ cab stand	Bushaltestelle [bus-hal-te-'shtell-e]/ Taxistand ['tak-si- shtant]
parking lot/parking garage	Parkplatz ['park-plats]/Parkhaus ['park-hows]
street map/map	Stadtplan ['shtat-plan]/Landkarte ['lant-kaa-te]
airport/train station	Flughafen ['floog-ha-fen]/ Bahnhof ['baan-hoaf]
schedule/ticket	Fahrplan ['faa-plan]/Fahrschein ['faa-shein]
I would like to rent ...	Ich möchte ... mieten [ikh 'mer-khte ... 'mee-ten]
a car/a bicycle	ein Auto [ein 'ow-to]/ein Fahrrad [ein 'faa-raat]
a motorhome/RV	ein Wohnmobil [ein 'vone-mo-beel]
a boat	ein Boot [ein 'boat]

petrol/gas station	Tankstelle ['tank-shtell-e]
petrol/gas / diesel	Benzin [ben-'tseen]/Diesel ['dee-zel]
breakdown/repair shop	Panne ['pan-e]/Werkstatt ['verk-shtat]

FOOD & DRINK

Could you please book a table for tonight for four?	Reservieren Sie uns bitte für heute Abend einen Tisch für vier Personen [rez-er-'vee-ren zee uns 'bi-te für 'hoy-te 'aa-bent 'ein-en tish für feer pair-'zo-nen]
The menu, please	Die Speisekarte, bitte [dee 'shpei-ze-kaa-te 'bi-te]
Could I please have ...?	Könnte ich ... haben? ['kern-te ihk ... 'haa-ben]
with/without ice/ sparkling	mit [mit]/ohne Eis ['oh-ne eis]/ Kohlensäure ['koh-len-zoy-re]
vegetarian/allergy	Vegetarier(in) [veg-e-'taa-ree-er]/Allergie [al-air-'gee]
May I have the bill, please?	Ich möchte zahlen, bitte [ikh 'merkh-te 'tsaa-len 'bi-te]

SHOPPING

Where can I find...?	Wo finde ich ...? [vo 'fin-de ikh]
I'd like .../I'm looking for ...	Ich möchte ... [ikh 'merkh-te]/Ich suche ... [ikh 'zoo-khe]
pharmacy/chemist	Apotheke [a-po-'tay-ke]/Drogerie [dro-ge-'ree]
shopping centre	Einkaufszentrum [ein-kowfs-'tsen-trum]
expensive/cheap/price	teuer ['toy-er]/billig ['bil-ig]/Preis [preis]
more/less	mehr [mayr]/weniger ['vay-ni-ger]
organically grown	aus biologischem Anbau [ows bee-o-'lo-gish-em 'an-bow]

ACCOMMODATION

I have booked a room	Ich habe ein Zimmer reserviert [ikh 'haa-be ein 'tsi-me rez-erv-'eert]
Do you have any ... left?	Haben Sie noch ein ... ['haa-ben zee nokh]
single room	Einzelzimmer ['ein-tsel-tsi-mer]
double room	Doppelzimmer ['dop-el-tsi-mer]
breakfast/half board	Frühstück ['frü-shtük]/Halbpension ['halp-pen-si-ohn]
full board	Vollpension ['foll-pen-si-ohn]
shower/sit-down bath	Dusche ['doo-she]/Bad [baat]
balcony/terrasse	Balkon [bal-'kohn]/Terrasse [te-'rass-e]
key/room card	Schlüssel ['shlü-sel]/Zimmerkarte ['tsi-mer-kaa-te]
luggage/suitcase	Gepäck [ge-'pek]/Koffer ['koff-er]/Tasche ['ta-she]

BANKS, MONEY & CREDIT CARDS

bank/ATM	Bank/Geldautomat [bank/'gelt-ow-to-maat]
pin code	Geheimzahl [ge-'heim-tsaal]
I'd like to change ...	Ich möchte ... wechseln [ikh 'merkh-te ... 'vek-seln]

| cash/credit card | bar [bar]/Kreditkarte [kre-'dit-kaa-te] |
| bill/coin | Banknote ['bank-noh-te]/Münze ['mün-tse] |

HEALTH

doctor/dentist/ paediatrician	Arzt [aatst]/Zahnarzt ['tsaan-aatst]/ Kinderarzt ['kin-der-aatst]
hospital/ emergency clinic	Krankenhaus ['kran-ken-hows]/ Notfallpraxis ['note-fal-prak-sis]
fever/pain	Fieber ['fee-ber]/Schmerzen ['shmer-tsen]
diarrhoea/nausea	Durchfall ['doorkh-fal]/Übelkeit ['ü-bel-keit]
inflamed/injured	entzündet [ent-'tsün-det]/verletzt [fer-'letst]
prescription	Rezept [re-'tsept]
pain reliever/tablet	Schmerzmittel ['shmerts-mit-el]/Tablette [ta-'blet-e]

POST, TELECOMMUNICATIONS & MEDIA

stamp/letter	Briefmarke ['brief-maa-ke]/Brief [brief]
postcard	Postkarte ['posst-kaa-te]
I'm looking for a prepaid card for my mobile	Ich suche eine Prepaid-Karte für mein Handy [ikh 'zoo-khe 'ei-ne 'pre-paid-kaa-te für mein 'hen-dee]
Do I need a special area code?	Brauche ich eine spezielle Vorwahl? ['brow-khe ikh 'ei-ne shpets-ee-'ell-e 'fore-vaal]
Where can I find internet access?	Wo finde ich einen Internetzugang? [vo 'fin-de ikh 'ei-nen 'in-ter-net-tsoo-gang]
socket/adapter/ charger/wi-fi	Steckdose ['shtek-doh-ze]/Adapter [a-'dap-te]/ Ladegerät ['laa-de-ge-rayt]/WLAN ['vay-laan]

LEISURE, SPORTS & BEACH

bike/scooter rental	Fahrrad-['faa-raat]/Mofa-Verleih ['mo-fa fer-lei]
rental shop	Vermietladen [fer-'meet-laa-den]
lesson	Übungsstunde ['ü-bungs-shtun-de]

NUMBERS

0 null [null]	10 zehn [tsayn]	20 zwanzig ['tsvantsikh]
1 eins [eins]	11 elf [elf]	50 Fünfzig ['fünf-tsikh]
2 zwei [tsvei]	12 zwölf [tsvölf]	100 (ein) Hundert ['hun-dert]
3 drei [drei]	13 dreizehn [' dreitsayn]	200 Zwei Hundert [tsvei 'hun-dert]
4 vier [feer]	14 vierzehn ['feertsayn]	1000 (ein) Tausend ['tow-zent]
5 fünf [fünf]	15 fünfzehn ['fünftsayn]	2000 Zwei Tausend [tsvei 'tow-zent]
6 sechs [zex]	16 sechzehn ['zekhtsayn]	10 000 Zehn Tausend [tsayn 'tow-zent]
7 sieben ['zeeben]	17 siebzehn ['zeebtsayn]	
8 acht [akht]	18 achtzehn ['akhtsayn]	½ ein halb [ein halp]
9 neun [noyn]	19 neunzehn ['noyntsayn]	¼ ein viertel [ein 'feer-tel]

NOTES

MARCO POLO TRAVEL GUIDES

ALGARVE
AMSTERDAM
ATHENS
AUSTRALIA
AUSTRIA
BANGKOK
BARCELONA
BERLIN
BRAZIL
BRUGES, GHENT &
  ANTWERP
BRUSSELS
BUDAPEST
BULGARIA
CALIFORNIA
CAMBODIA
CANADA EAST
CANADA WEST
  ROCKIES
CAPE TOWN
  WINE LANDS,
  GARDEN ROUTE
CAPE VERDE
CHANNEL ISLANDS
CHICAGO
  & THE LAKES
CHINA
COLOGNE
COPENHAGEN
CORFU
COSTA BLANCA
  VALENCIA
COSTA BRAVA
  BARCELONA
COSTA DEL SOL
  GRANADA
CRETE
CUBA
CYPRUS
  NORTH AND
  SOUTH
DUBAI
DUBLIN
DUBROVNIK &
  DALMATIAN COAST
EDINBURGH

EGYPT
EGYPT'S RED
  SEA RESORTS
FINLAND
FLORENCE
FLORIDA
FRENCH ATLANTIC
  COAST
FRENCH RIVIERA
  NICE, CANNES &
  MONACO
FUERTEVENTURA
GRAN CANARIA
GREECE
HAMBURG
HONG KONG
  MACAU
ICELAND
INDIA
INDIA SOUTH
  GOA & KERALA
IRELAND
ISRAEL
ISTANBUL
ITALY
JORDAN
KOS
KRAKOW
LAKE GARDA

LANZAROTE
LAS VEGAS
LISBON
LONDON
LOS ANGELES
MADEIRA
  PORTO SANTO
MADRID
MALLORCA
MALTA
  GOZO
MAURITIUS
MENORCA
MILAN
MOROCCO
MUNICH
NAPLES &
  THE AMALFI COAST
NEW YORK
NEW ZEALAND
NORWAY
OSLO
PARIS
PHUKET
PORTUGAL
PRAGUE

RHODES
ROME
SAN FRANCISCO
SARDINIA
SCOTLAND
SEYCHELLES
SHANGHAI
SICILY
SINGAPORE
SOUTH AFRICA
STOCKHOLM
SWITZERLAND
TENERIFE
THAILAND
TURKEY
TURKEY
  SOUTH COAST
TUSCANY
UNITED ARAB
  EMIRATES
USA SOUTHWEST
VENICE
VIENNA
VIETNAM

- PACKED WITH INSIDER TIPS
- BEST WALKS AND TOURS
- FULL-COLOUR PULL-OUT MAP
  AND STREET ATLAS

STREET ATLAS

The green line ▬▬▬ indicates the Walking tours (p. 100–105)

All tours are also marked on the pull-out map

Photo: Elbe with a view of the city's landmark, the 'Michel'

Exploring Hamburg

The map on the back cover shows how the area has been sub-divided

CAP SAN DIEGO

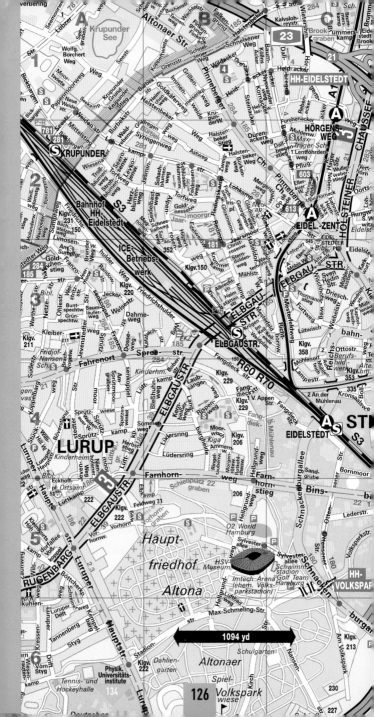

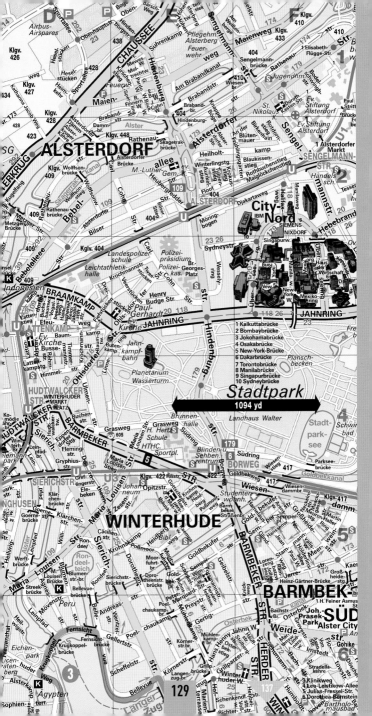

Stadtpark

1094 yd

1 Kalkuttabrücke
2 Bombaybrücke
3 Jokohamabrücke
4 Osakabrücke
5 New-York-Brücke
6 Dakarbrücke
7 Torontobrücke
8 Manilabrücke
9 Singapurbrücke
10 Sydneybrücke

ALSTERDORF

City-Nord
IBM
SIEMENS
NIXDORF

BRAAMKAMP

JAHNRING

HUDTWALCKER

WINTERHUDE

BARMBEK

BARMBEK-SÜD
Alster City

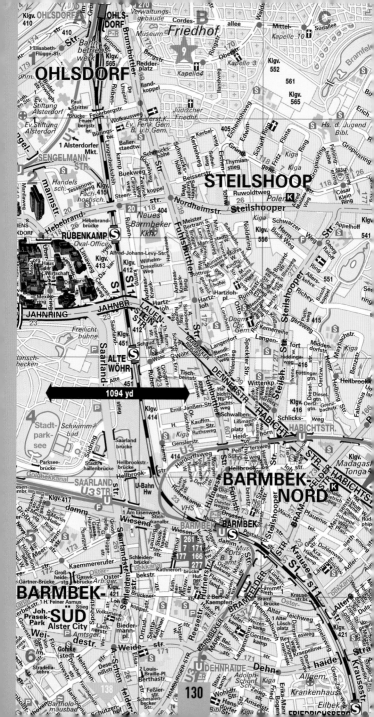

Hyperboloid projection (magnifying glass effect): Change of scale from the inner city to the outlying districts

This page is a map showing the districts of OSDORF, GROSS FLOTTBEK, HOCHKAMP, NIENSTEDTEN, OTHMARSCHEN, KLEIN FLOTTBEK, and surrounding areas, with the river Elbe and Teufelsbrück.

Map labels include:

OK

OSDORF

GROSS FLOTTBEK

HOCHKAMP

Zentr. für Schulbiologie und Umwelterziehung

Loki-Schmidt-Garten

Inst.f. Allgem. Botanik

Polo-platz

HOCHKAMPhuden

NIEN-STEDTEN

Nienstedtener Friedhf.

KLEIN FLOTTBEK

Klein Flottbek
1 Am Klein Flottbeker Bhf.

OTHMAR-SCHEN

Jenisch-Haus

Jenisch-NSG Flottbek-tal park

Otto Ernst Christia-neum

Großflottbeker Tennis-, Hockey- u. Golf-Club e.V.

Ernst Barlach Haus

Hochrad

Meitner-Park
Groß Flottbek

Elbe Einkaufs Zentr.

Waitzstr.
1 Hermann-Niebuhr-Weg

1 Lübbersmeyerweg
2 Harderweg
3 H.-Christian-Andersen-Park

E l b e

Teufelsbrück
1 Teufelsbrück

Teufelsbrück

1094 yd

Flugzeugwerft
Deutsche
Aerospace

AIRBUS

Hyperboloid projection (magnifying glass effect): Change of scale from the inner city to the outlying districts

E40
1705 2703 2704
2706-08 2718
2711-13 2719
4710 4714-17
4700 4701

TUHH
Technologie-zentr.

Neßdeich

Rüschpark

Gorch-Fock-Park

Seemanns sch.

133

21 39
E86

36 E86

Hans Leip

Hindenbu park

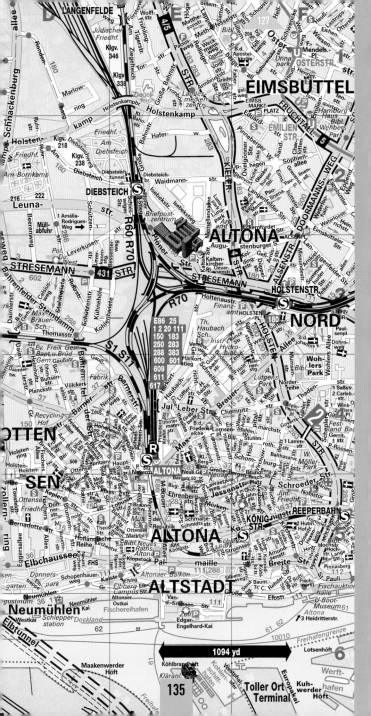

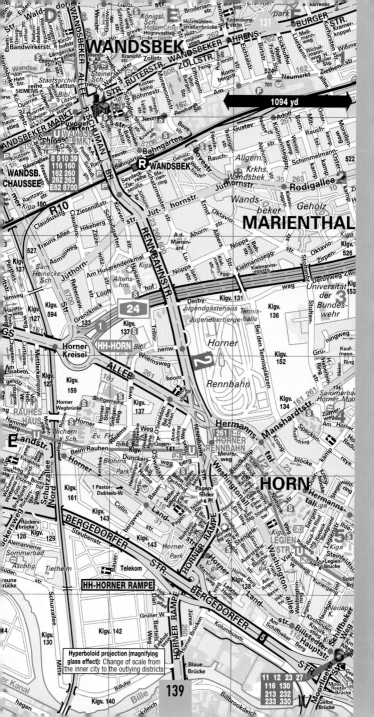

Hyperboloid projection (magnifying glass effect): Change of scale from the inner city to the outlying districts.

139

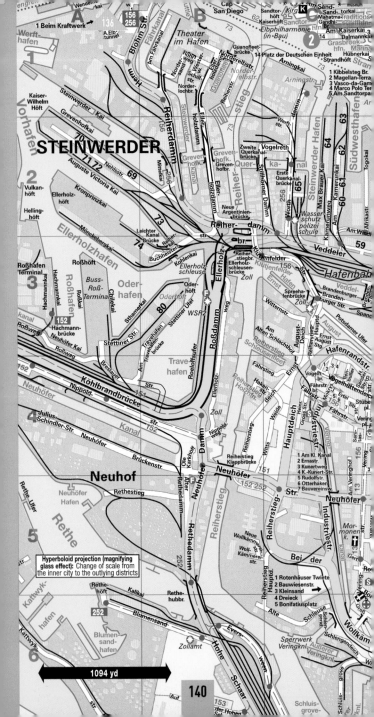

Hyperboloid projection (magnifying glass effect): Change of scale from the inner city to the outlying districts

1094 yd

140

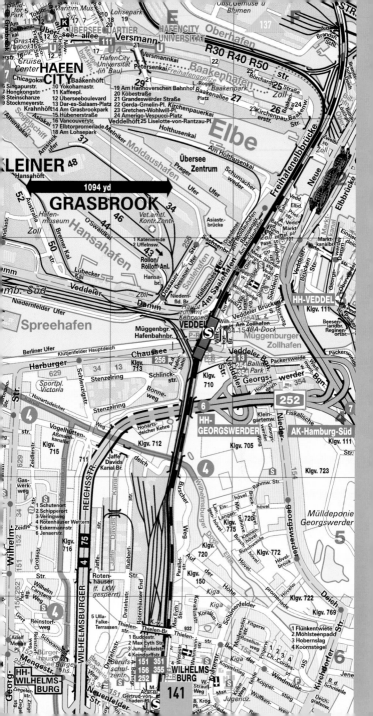

This index lists a selection of the streets and squares shown in the street atlas

KEY TO STREET ATLAS

Built-up area Bebaute Fläche	Terrain bâti	
Public Building Öffentliche Gebäude	Bâtiment public	
Industrial area Industriegelände	Zone industrielle	
Wood Wald　Bois	**Park** Park　Parc	
Sports fiels Sportplatz Terrain de sports	**Allotment ground** Kleingarten Jardins particuliers	
Motorway Autobahn Autoroute	**Motorroad** Schnellstraße Route à plusieurs voies	
National road Bundestraße	Route nationale	
Main road Hauptstraße	Route principale	
Railway Eisenbahn	Chemin de fer	
Suburban railway S-Bahn	Train regional	
Underground U-Bahn	Métro	
One way street Einbahnstraße	Sens unique	
Bus route Buslinie	Autobus	

Pedestrian precinct Fußgängerzone	Zone piétonne	
Adm. District Boundary Bezirksgrenze	Limite des district	
Church Kirche	Église	
Post office Post	Bureau de poste	
Police station Polizeiwache	Poste de Police	
Hospital Krankenhaus	Hôpital	
School Schule	École	
Fire station Feuerwache	Poste de pompiers	
Park & Ride Parkplatz an S- und U-Bahnhöfen		
Theatre Theater	Théâtre	
Indoor swimming pool Hallenbad	Piscine couverte	
Open-air swimming pool Freibad	Piscine de plain air	
Information centre Informationsbüro	Bureau de renseignements	

Walking tour
Stadtspaziergang　Promenade en ville

MARCO POLO Highlight
MARCO POLO Highlight

Hyperboloid-projection (magnifying effect)

The map projection brings about a change of scale from the city centre to the outlying districts. Consequently the city centre is presented in a more readable form (magnifying glass effect). The black arrows are to estimate distances; the length of each arrow represents 1km/0.62mi.

INDEX

This index lists all sights and destinations plus the names of important streets, places, people and keywords featured in this guide. Numbers in bold indicate a main entry.

WRITE TO US

e-mail: info@marcopologuides.co.uk

Did you have a great holiday?
Is there something on your mind?
Whatever it is, let us know!
Whether you want to praise, alert us to errors or give us a personal tip – MARCO POLO would be pleased to hear from you.
We do everything we can to provide the very latest information for your trip.

Nevertheless, despite all of our authors' thorough research, errors can creep in. MARCO POLO does not accept any liability for this. Please contact us by e-mail or post.

MARCO POLO Travel Publishing Ltd
Pinewood, Chineham Business Park
Crockford Lane, Chineham
Basingstoke, Hampshire RG24 8AL
United Kingdom

PICTURE CREDITS
Cover photograph: Speicherstadt (Huber: Gräfenhain)
DuMont Bildarchiv: Schröder (106/107, 108/109, 149); © fotolia.com: Thomas Berg (16 top), spuno (17 top); HAM.LIT: Benedikt Schnermann (16 centre); A. Honert (1 bottom); Huber: Gräfenhain (1 top, 2 centre bottom, 26/27, 56, 68 left, 110 top); I. Knigge (95); Laif: Gaasterland (50), Multhaupt (3 centre, 80/81), Selbach (3 bottom, 8, 90/91, 92, 96); Look: Engel & Gielen (45); mauritius images: imagebroker.net (55), Waldkirch (21); Mutterland: Björn Jarosch (16 bottom); mylys: Ray Nher (17 bottom); D. Renckhoff (2 top, 2 bottom, 3 top, 4, 5, 6, 15, 40/41, 42, 47, 53, 58, 60/61, 62, 65, 66, 69, 71, 72/73, 74, 76, 79, 82, 85, 87, 88, 98, 100/101, 107, 108, 110 bottom, 111); White Star: Pasdzior (31, 37, 51, 106), Reichelt (109); M. Zapf (front flap left, front flap right, 2 centre top, 7, 9, 10/11, 12/13, 18/19, 22/23, 24 left, 24 right, 25, 32, 34, 39, 48, 68 right, 102, 104, 122/123)

1st Edition 2014
Worldwide Distribution: Marco Polo Travel Publishing Ltd, Pinewood, Chineham Business Park, Crockford Lane, Basingstoke, Hampshire RG24 8AL, United Kingdom. E-mail: sales@marcopolouk.com
© MAIRDUMONT GmbH & Co. KG, Ostfildern
Chief editor: Marion Zorn
Author: Dorothea Heintze; editor: Jochen Schürmann
Programme supervision: Ann-Katrin Kutzner, Nikolai Michaelis
Picture editors: Gabriele Forst, Stefan Scholtz
What's hot: wunder media, Munich
Cartography street atlas; Cartography pull-out map: © MAIRDUMONT, Ostfildern
Design: milchhof: atelier, Berlin; Front cover, pull-out map cover, page 1: factor product munich
Translated from German by Tony Halliday; editor of the English edition: Margaret Howie, fullproof.co.za
Prepress: M. Feuerstein, Wigel
Phrase book in cooperation with Ernst Klett Sprachen GmbH, Stuttgart, Editorial by Pons Wörterbücher.

DOS & DON'TS ✋

A few things to bear in mind on your holiday

DON'T PARK IN THE WRONG PLACE

For landlubbers the car parks right on the banks of the Elbe, for example at the Fischmarkt in Altona or Övelgönne, may look completely safe and dry. But floods can happen quickly and sometimes unexpectedly, and the police are not always on hand to tow away vehicles. Don't leave your car there for too long unattended, and heed the warnings!

DON'T LEAVE RUBBISH ON THE BEACHES

On balmy summer evenings, the beaches along the Elbe in Övelgönne and Wittenbergen are full of little fires, portable barbecues and young people strumming guitars. The whole thing is wonderfully romantic – though it's not officially allowed but just tolerated – but please light your fire only where it is allowed and don't leave your rubbish behind!

DO BEHAVE ON THE REEPERBAHN

Of course you want to go to the Reeperbahn – and you should – but try to follow a few written, and unwritten, rules. Don't try the patience of the professional ladies in the side streets; they have a job to do, just like the rest of us. Weapons of all kinds are forbidden and you are not allowed to drink out of glass bottles on the street at the weekend. The police react quickly and show no tolerance.

DON'T MOAN ABOUT THE WEATHER

Yes, of course the weather could be better. The people of Hamburg know that themselves. But what's the point of moaning about it? A better idea is to take a raincoat and pullover with you and try to be optimistic! Even the lowest-lying, leaden clouds have a silver lining.

DO WATCH OUT

Nowhere is it really dangerous in Hamburg, unless you start trouble at night on the Reeperbahn (known colloquially as the 'Kiez') or in around Hansaplatz in St Georg. Be that as it may, Hamburg is a big city and pickpockets are everywhere, particularly in those places where there are jostling crowds, such as the Fischmarkt. Keep an eye on your belongings!

DO BE ALERT WHEN WALKING OR DRIVING

Many strangers to the city have almost had a heart attack when, walking innocently along the pavement, they are suddenly overtaken – within a whisker and without any warning – by a cyclist going at breakneck speed. In Hamburg cyclists are allowed to ride on many pavements and they are often quite inconsiderate. Keep your eyes open when you are driving too: cyclists are allowed to ride down many one-way streets in the opposite direction.